ENTERING THE TWO

BY THE SAME AUTHOR

The Shattering of Loneliness

ENTERING THE TWOFOLD MYSTERY

On Christian Conversion

ERIK VARDEN

BLOOMSBURY CONTINUUM
LONDON · OXFORD · NEW YORK · NEW DELHI · SYDNEY

BLOOMSBURY CONTINUUM
50 Bedford Square, London, WC1B 3DP, UK
29 Earlsfort Terrace, Dublin 2, Ireland

BLOOMSBURY, BLOOMSBURY CONTINUUM and the Diana logo are
trademarks of Bloomsbury Publishing Plc

First published in Great Britain 2022

A catalogue record for this book is available from the British Library

Library of Congress Cataloguing-in-Publication data has been applied for

ISBN: TPB: 978-1-4729-7947-6; eBook: 978-1-4729-7944-5;
ePDF: 978-1-4729-7945-2

2 4 6 8 10 9 7 5 3 1

Typeset by by Deanta Global Publishing Services, Chennai, India
Printed and bound in Great Britain by CPI Group (UK) Ltd,
Croydon CR0 4YY

MIX
Paper from
responsible sources
FSC® C171272

To find out more about our authors and books visit www.bloomsbury.com
and sign up for our newsletters

CONTENTS

LIST OF ILLUSTRATIONS

Solo chi ama conosce. Povero chi non ama!
Come a sguardi inconsacrati le ostie sante,
comuni e spoglie sono per lui le mille vite.
Solo a chi ama il Diverso accende i suoi splendori
e gli si apre la casa dei due misteri:
il mistero doloroso e il mistero gaudioso.

Elsa Morante

Introduction

We speak too readily, perhaps, of 'life-changing' experiences. To really change a life is harder than we like to admit. A powerful catalyst is called for. Even with this proviso, there is an incident without which I should not have been the same. It woke me up when I needed waking. It provided the final impetus I needed to abandon the beaten track and set off into the unknown, to begin to become a monk.

It occurred one evening in December 2001. I was living in Paris, doing post-doctoral research. I had a job waiting for me at Cambridge. I was comfortable, engaged in absorbing work, free to direct it as I chose in a city I loved, surrounded by kind, interesting people. Yet I was consumed by emptiness within. Without being able to say why, I felt the life I was living did not correspond to what I was supposed to live. I had an uncomfortable sense of play-acting, of being a fraud, simply by virtue of getting on with my life as it was.

That evening, I had been out dining with friends. We had been to the cinema, I think, and had gone to eat afterwards. We were ambling back along a boulevard at midnight, sufficiently fuelled not to feel the chill. There was snow in the air. I can't remember what we talked about, but we were cheerful, carefree. I returned to my lodgings content.

I was staying in a room let by the Dominicans of the Annunciation Priory on the Rue du Faubourg Saint-Honoré, rich in Proustian associations. The street is one of the most expensive in Paris, a five-minute walk from the Arc de Triomphe. The friars' next-door neighbour was – still is – a champagne merchant's. Across the street lay a restaurant with frosted windows patronized by glamorous politicians. I was fumbling sleepily with my keys when I realized there was an obstacle in front of the main door.

A tramp was lying in a sleeping bag right along the threshold. I felt a surge of panic, then something akin to anger. What should I do? I am not proud to say I needed to take a turn around the block to answer that question. My wish was to be undisturbed. Why should this common tramp interfere with my comfortable and (in my own eyes) vaguely distinguished existence? Why could he not have settled in front of someone else's front door?

Thus spoke one voice in my head. Another voice tempered it. It reminded me that I called myself a Christian, after all; that my intention was to go to my room, clean my teeth, then kneel by my bed to pray. Could I do that having first stepped over a poor man's body? I decided I couldn't, even for pragmatic reasons: I wouldn't have been able to sleep. I composed myself and went back to the doorway, said a prayer, put a hand on the man's shoulder and roused him.

He was not pleased. He had managed to escape from the cold into sleep's embrace, and cursed me for bringing him back. It took him a while to come to. We began a tentative conversation. I said I would like to help him find a room for the night. He looked up, but did not say anything. I said I didn't have much cash, which was true, but that I could get more, should my 100 francs not suffice. He looked me in the eyes, and said, 'That's more than enough.' 'Do you know where to go?' I asked. He said, 'Yes.' He began to extract himself from his sleeping bag. As he pulled down the zip, I saw it contained bits of food. I remember an opened pack of sliced ham, a tin of something. I could see the bag was wet with urine. The man, who must have been about my age, say 25, was unsteady on his feet. I wasn't sure he would manage to walk very well, so asked if I might accompany him. He said casually, 'If you like.'

As we walked, the tone of our conversation changed. I had from the first addressed him with the formal pronoun *vous*. He had brusquely responded with *tu*. Now he changed to the polite form. He spoke about himself, unsentimentally, though with reserve. He said he had been living on the street for years. He referred obliquely to a painful situation at home. Then he began to talk about his friends. He became eloquent. 'Do you know', he asked, 'that last year, here in Paris, a dozen people died on the street, having frozen to death?' I did not know.

While we talked we walked through a neighbourhood I thought of as familiar. But I saw it as if for the first time, as if through disenchanted spectacles. There were features I had never noticed. My companion pointed to a pile of cardboard in an alley and said, 'There's Monique.' Further on, he indicated a dark shape behind a rubbish bin and said, 'And there's Jean, asleep.' I was made aware of inhabiting a landscape more densely populated than I had realized, full of otherwise invisible people. My companion told me their names. In his face

I could glimpse their faces. He said emphatically, '*Voilà, Monsieur, voilà la misère!*' I wanted to weep. I asked if I might know his own name? He looked at me and said, 'Manu – well, Emmanuel.'

As we moved along, Manu's pace became brisker, more regular. I began to wonder if I would find my way home. I asked where we were going? He pointed to a brightly lit street, saying, 'A friend of mine works that street. She will get me a room.' I said I would have to start making my way back. We stopped to take our leave. We looked at each other. The moment was strangely solemn. With grace, Manu took my hand and shook it. He said, '*Monsieur, je vous respecte* ... And I hope', he added, 'that, one day, you and I will sit down and have a glass together.' Remember, it was Advent. As I left Emmanuel to seek out his Magdalene, those words could not fail to resonate with eternity.

My heart, previously dark, was charged with a joy so profound it was painful. Walking home, I was inundated with light. Though did I walk? I felt I was dancing, like a character out of Woody Allen's absurd but delightful Parisian reverie, *Everyone Says I Love You*: so light had I become. I knew that that night had revealed something to me. In the language of Luke's Gospel, I had 'seen' a 'word' (Luke 2.15, in the Greek text). Emmanuel, whose name means 'God with us' (Matthew 1.23), had become for me an angel, that is, a messenger. He had opened my eyes to humanity hurting, frightened, yet able, in a flash, to rise to immense dignity. His handshake had been to me an ennobling pledge. Oh, to be worthy of it! I thought of the ancient Celtic rune: 'Oft, oft, oft, goes the Christ in a stranger's guise.'

I felt commissioned there and then to answer for the misery and greatness I had seen. It was clear to me that, somehow, I must respond by devoting my life, poor as it was, to intercession for the world in union with the sacrifice of Christ, by which the weight of our condition is raised up, redeemed, and tinged with glory. I knew my task was, in this way, to breathe hope into our too often hopeless world. Nothing seemed more urgent to me then. To this day, nothing seems more urgent.

And so I think of Manu with gratitude. I count him among the great teachers I have known. I pray for him, wondering whether he still walks the streets of Paris or is seated at table in the Father's house? Whatever the case may be, I trust we shall have that glass together one day, he and I.

Within the mystery of the Church, we dare to believe that a Christian life truly given may, by God's providence, be an effective balm on the wounds of the poor of our world, who are given us to carry and nurture. Such oblative living does not substitute for practical assistance; but without this personal, engaged, even mystical dimension, no amount of sandwiches and soup will ever have a truly transformative effect. This insight poses a challenge for all of us.

'My brother,' said St Silouan of Mount Athos, a great monk of the twentieth century, 'is my life.'[1] His words remind us that the incarnation of the Word set in motion a radical redefinition of relationships that will slowly transform our very sense of self. We are summoned to rise to full stature, to perform with generosity and grace the mission allotted to each one of us in God's design for the redemption of the world. If we pay close attention, we may become alert to the sound of angels' voices calling to us from afar, or even from very near.

The pieces collected here are talks and homilies given at Mount Saint Bernard Abbey while I was privileged to serve as abbot there. They are attempts to record fugitive chords of the music I heard that night on a street in Paris, when the firmament seemed to open, and which I then kept listening out for, with and through my brothers, in the monastery. Monastic life aspires to embody the angelic *Gloria* in such a way that all things reveal their glorious potential.[2] The monk seeks constantly to be converted, that is, to be reoriented, turning with determination from darkness to light, from falsehood to truth, from westward mirages in the desert sand to the Sun of Righteousness that rises in the East with healing in its wings (Malachi 4.2). He would make of his life a ladder like the one Jacob saw in a dream (Genesis 28.12), singing as he ascends, uniting earth and heaven in consonance. If this book makes occasional harmonies audible, I give thanks.

PART ONE

WHAT MAKES A MONK

1

Vows

OBEDIENCE: TO LEARN TO BE FREE

As monks, our lives are structured by a covenant. The terms of that covenant are three vows. The first is our vow of obedience. It represents a counter-cultural commitment, to say the least, in times fiercely attached to notions of autonomy. What does it mean to be 'autonomous'? Literally, 'to be a law unto oneself'. Aspirations to autonomy can be noble and good. In eighteenth- and nineteenth-century Europe, ideologies of autonomy arose in response to injustice, social inequality and the abuse of what we now consider inalienable human rights. The call for autonomy was launched as a battle cry against servitude, an affirmation of the human person's right to form his or her destiny. None of us would quarrel with that.

Other pursuits of autonomy are more ambiguous. Think of advertising's rhetoric of entitlement. How often are we not told we 'deserve' this thing or that: an unhealthy dessert, some gadgetry, a nice holiday? 'You have a right to realize your desires.' That is the gospel of marketing. If we believe it, only a small step keeps us from a promise more ambitious still, which tells us: 'You can become what you like.'

This assumption has saturated Western consciousness to such an extent that our society suffers from chronic discontent. Why? Because it cannot be realized. We are told we are supreme masters of our fate. If we like (and have money), we can change the way we live, look and talk. We can change our name and nationality, even our gender. Computers set up for multiple users prompt us to change 'identity'. Many people seek to realize that virtual transformation in real life. It is bound to fail. Sooner or later we run into circumstances beyond our control. We encounter ourselves as we are: limited, vulnerable, mortal. Unprepared for setbacks, we respond with anger, feeling like the victims of a breach of contract.

This second, spurious kind of autonomy contradicts a fundamental principle of Christian anthropology, already spelt out in the Old Testament. I'd say this largely explains the visceral hostility of post-Christian Europe to the claims of religion. The religious person constructs his life on the certainty that he is *not* autonomous, and glories in it. Happiness, he knows, is a function of dependence; true freedom, for him, is found through obedience. To a secular way of thinking this sounds outrageous. Is obedience not the antithesis of freedom? Let us consider why our answer to that question must be 'No'.

Human self-understanding in the Jewish-Christian tradition is founded on the twenty-seventh verse of the first chapter of the Book of Genesis: 'And God created man in his own image, in the image of God created He him, male and female created He them.' God, we know, is Spirit. He cannot be bound by time and space. He cannot be contained in matter. Yet with the creation of man, he leaves an imprint of himself in the temporal, spatial reality of our world. The human being is to be a sign of divinity in creation, a bridge between time and eternity.

Learned, holy men and women have asked themselves for three thousand years what it means to be made 'in the image of God'. The array of theories on offer need not detain us now. We can content ourselves with what is obvious. To be created 'in the image' of God is to exist on the basis of a relationship. It is to be constituted in such a way that our being and flourishing depend on a power outside ourselves that exceeds us infinitely. This relational nature of man – the fact that we are, by definition, incomplete in ourselves – lies at the heart of religious obedience.

A stone is a stone. Its stoniness does not depend on any outside force. Plants carry in themselves a code for growth ('fruit wherein is the seed thereof', we read in Genesis 1.12); they develop after a fixed pattern. Animals are conditioned by instinct. Human beings function differently. They can weigh up alternatives and make choices. As a function of the divine image in which they are made, they possess the privilege of freedom. For that reason they have something to give that other creatures do not have. They can make a free gift of themselves.

Why was Adam given a commandment in Eden? Why did God make it possible for him to *dis*obey? Because only thus could Adam choose to direct his will according to the will of another and freely embrace the good. Think about it: our freedom is the one thing we can truly call our own. In every other respect, our being

21

is contingent. The only offering we can make to our Maker is the offering of our freedom. The dietary law of paradise, the law of the forbidden fruit, was intended to test how man would use this privilege.

By obeying God's commandment, Adam would have shown that he trusted his Maker. His trust would have been a first expression of love. By obeying God, he could own the truth of himself as made in God's image. By self-giving he would have received himself. There is not a trace of degradation in such obedience. On the contrary, it is regal and ennobling. Ephrem the Syrian gives a wonderful perspective on the original invitation to obey. 'Like a priest with fragrant incense,' he says, 'Adam's keeping of the commandment was to be his censer.'[3] It was to be an act of praise, a liturgy of worship.

Things turned out differently. What we know of the Fall from Scripture, we verify daily through experience. But the original relationship of trust for which God intended us has not been cancelled by our infidelity. In the wake of Christ's sacrifice, the door to Eden stands open. The fact that we are here, in this monastery, is proof that we hope to enter the garden and stay. The path of obedience takes us there.

What, then, does it mean to obey? Religious obedience is first of all a confession of faith. By obeying what I understand to be God's will, I acknowledge that my life depends on God; that he has made me, knows what is good for me, and would have me live in intimate union with himself. To obey him is to be established in an ecstatic relation, as I look to God for the fulfilment of my deepest longing.

To obey is to live in a state of sonship. It is to confess with the full force of my freedom that I have an infinitely good Father who loves me with infinite love.[4] By obeying him I realize the extent of my freedom and find that it grows ever more immense. On the burning coals of free self-giving, even humdrum duties release a fragrance of adoration, becoming priestly acts of grandeur, sweet incense burnt in the censer of obedience. As long as we keep swinging it, our entire life becomes a liturgy of praise, an oblation of love. That is the bottom line of religious obedience. It is an education in sonship, a workshop of responsibility, a school of true freedom.

About once a week, in the refectory, we pray in our grace after lunch that, like Christ, we may be made 'obedient unto death'. I am always stirred when I hear the words. There is something oddly appropriate about having this enormous proposition thrown at us outside the setting of solemn liturgy, in the noonday heat when, with a full stomach, we brace ourselves for the dishes and look forward to the deep sleep of midday. Our prayer cites the letter to the Philippians (2.8): 'Being found in human form he humbled himself and became obedient unto death, even death on a cross' – words that haunt the liturgy of Holy Week when, in the modulations of the antiphon '*Christus factus est*', it prepares our minds and hearts for the intensity, each year seemingly unbearable, of Good Friday.

Christ's Passion, his suffering and death on the cross, was the culmination of his surrender to the Father's will. That is obvious. But the obedience of Christ extends beyond Calvary into every aspect of his incarnate life. By considering some of its other manifestations, we may see how it impinges on our discipleship. For our pledge of 'obedience unto death' is not limited to the end of life. It calls for a constant death to self in small and ordinary ways that teach us what it means to make the life of Christ our own.

'And he went down with them and came to Nazareth, and was obedient to them.' That is how the interlude of the child Jesus lost in Jerusalem comes to an end in the Gospel of Luke (2.51). It is amazing: the incarnate Word, the Wisdom of the Father, yielded himself to the judgement of human parents. The two, Mary and Joseph, were no ordinary couple, but were fully human, thank God; and so their understanding and insight could not, by definition, match his.

Why did the Word made flesh submit to such constriction? Why did he not follow John's example and retire to the desert as a youth? He submitted, first of all, because these people had been given him by his heavenly Father as the means most apt to prepare him for his mission. Second, he obeyed for love. Loving them, knowing they loved him, Jesus entrusted his life to Mary and Joseph even if they could not plumb the depth of his mystery. To obey for love is an apt response to love. These, then, are the elements we intuit in the obedience of Nazareth: trust in the particular design of providence; trust in the carrying force of human love.

Christ's mature life, too, was marked by obedience. It is striking how, again and again, he yields to others' requests. Think of Peter's wife's mother, of the paralytic let down through the roof, of Jairus with his twelve-year-old, of the woman with a flow of blood. True, we have the example of the Syrophoenician mother who had to plead her case before she got what she wanted; but even here Jesus attended to her from the first, prepared to reason. His response was not a rejection but, it would seem, an expression of genuine perplexity.

So it is true to say that Christ responded with obedience to just about everyone who asked him for something. He did not cross-examine them first to make certain their motives were pure. No less impressive is his obedience to the lawgivers who 'sit on Moses' seat' (Matthew 23.2). In this respect, he observed the advice he gave others, so that the Church's later doctrine of *ex opere operato*, by which the efficacy of a sacrament is not held to depend on the minister's worthiness, can be traced to Christ's example. Grace and blessing, he reminds us, can flow through imperfect, even sullied human channels when the original design is of God. In the Church and in monastic life, this is a mystery to ponder often.

Throughout John's Gospel, we hear Jesus invoking the imperative of 'the Father's will' with an intensity that grows as he approaches Calvary: 'I have come to you in my Father's name' (5.43); 'I seek not my own will but the will of him who sent me' (6.38); 'You, Father, are in me, and I in you' (17.21). The sublime theology of later centuries enables us to form some notion of the Son's eternal being as a response in obedience to the Father's eternal love: a surrender so total that no human reality can indicate it adequately.

It is this transcendent, divine abandonment that raises Christ up on the cross, charging it with 'glory'. The lesson for us is clear. The obedience asked of us in great things and in small is no end in itself. It is a pedagogy intended to teach a new mode of living and relating, a quality of trust that cannot be rationalized, but pertains to the realm of faith. Only by schooling in such trust shall we be prepared to enter into the divine relations that constitute eternal life, for which we hope with all our hearts. Obedience is an apprenticeship for beatitude.

We can only pray to become obedient like Christ if we remain resolutely obedient to Christ. This personal submission of our lives to the lordship of Christ is not specific to the monastic state. It is part of every Christian's baptismal covenant. The Fathers insisted on this point. Often enough, they embraced monastic life for pragmatic reasons, because it seemed to provide props that made it less impossible to maintain a commitment already made. When St Anthony the Great heard the Gospel of the Rich Young Man, it affected him as it did because he knew it was really about himself.[5] He was already a Christian; he had put his hand on the plough. Had he any other choice than to carry on determinedly ahead? Abba Gregory gives voice to the same insight in different terms. He used to say that, 'God asks three things of anyone who is baptised: to keep the true faith with all his soul and all his might; to control his tongue; to be chaste in his body.'[6] When he retired to the desert, it was in large measure because he could see no other way of living up to his destiny.

This begs questions of us, questions that are not always comfortable. Do I so fully live in the Spirit that I can say, with regard to every aspect of my life, 'Jesus is Lord'? Do I acknowledge Christ's lordship over my instincts and appetites? Or do I keep pockets sewn up for private use, indulging desires, dreams and imaginings I have formally renounced? Is Jesus Lord over my passions? Or do I sub-let areas to myself, breathing on embers of resentment, enjoying the bitter draught of anger? Is Jesus Christ – the same yesterday, today and for ever – Lord of my past and future? Or do I hug achievements, experiences, pleasures and hurts of distant years, while making plans for a tomorrow not my own? It is by examining ourselves in such terms that we shall find whether our profession of obedience is real or just the clanging of a gong. The Lord does not expect us to take up our cross in our own strength. He promises to carry it with us. He can do nothing, however, without our free gift of ourselves. That gift needs to be practised and refined constantly. It is the chief lesson we have come here – to the 'School of the Lord's service'[7] – to learn, so that, on graduation, we may be found to be vessels fit for a weight of glory.

The Rule of St Benedict sets out from two strong statements about obedience. They define the tenor of the Rule and its logic. The first occurs right at the beginning of the Prologue: 'The labour of obedience will bring you back to him from whom you had drifted through the sloth of disobedience.'[8] There are several things to note. First, the monastic life is presented as a journey of return. The monk is a prodigal son who recognizes himself as such. He knows he has lost his sense of direction. He knows he is far from the wellspring of life and joy, and that the cause of his misfortune is *dis*obedience, that is, failure to recognize what is truly good and to realize this good in concrete living.

Obedience is set before him as the way, the only way, back – to what? Not to some abstract ideal or order, but to a Person: 'to him from whom you had drifted'. To obey is to set out in pursuit of an encounter. It is to confess, with the totality of my being, that I am tired of pursuing some illusory bliss of my own invention. I want truth. I am no longer satisfied with reflections of goodness, glimpsed in puddles along the criss-crossed route my life has taken till now. I want Goodness itself. I want Him who is good.

This is the motivation St Benedict presupposes. It is as if he were saying to us: 'You know from experience that self-will does not cause you to flourish. Follow instead the path of obedience. I guarantee it will take you where you want to go.' The obedience proposed by the Rule is the opposite of an imposition. The obedient monk is not a belittled, servile creature, but one who knows what is good for him, and who has the courage to act on that knowledge. True, at the outset, 'labour' is called for. 'Sloth' has accustomed us to indolence, weighing down our spiritual faculties with unbecoming flabbiness. The workout of obedience restores us to shape. The better we perform it, the fitter we shall be to throw ourselves into the Father's embrace, restored to the freedom of sonship.

St Benedict's second statement, also from the Prologue, develops the same theme, but in terms of an enquiry. It constitutes a timeless 'mirror for monks', a touchstone on which we can assess our authenticity of observance. 'This message of mine is for you, then, if you are ready to give up your own will, once and for all, and armed with the strong and noble weapons of obedience to do battle for the true King, Christ the Lord.'[9] The key word in Benedict's Latin is the participle *abrenuntians*. It speaks of renunciation that, through the prefix *ab*, is rendered definitive. Our translation is justified in expanding a little and translating, 'give up your own will, once and for all'. The monk is to spend his life on the battlefield of the spirit. Compromises and half-resolutions will endanger both himself and his company. They could bring down the kingly banner under which he marches.

In community, we look to one another for inspiration and good example in this respect. The old look to the young, hoping to find in them the zeal and zest with which they set out long ago. The young look to the old to see whether their commitment still carries, whether they continue to wield the weapons of obedience with the confidence of victors. Once again St Benedict's choice of imagery is striking. Obedience to him is a soldierly virtue. It requires nobility of mind, uprightness of heart, strength of soul.

Even from this cursory account, we can identify the core of Benedictine obedience. It is a matter of submitting whim to will so that a deep, unifying, reasoned longing can gradually still the noise of myriad chaotic desires.

This basic orientation enables St Benedict to establish what I like to think of as three dimensions of obedience. In the Rule, these are linked to three key axioms. The first is listed in Chapter 4, where it summarizes all the other 'Tools for good works': 'Prefer nothing to the love of Christ.'[10] Perhaps we spontaneously interpret it in vertical terms, as pertaining to the individual's relationship with the Lord: 'Love Christ before all, and everyone, else. Let nothing come between you and him.' This is a true reading, certainly. But the horizontal application is no less fundamental: 'Let the love of

Christ be your guiding star in all you do. Let nothing – *nothing* – come before your practice of it.'

Bossuet, in his *Panegyric of St Benedict*, famously described the Rule as a 'distillation of the Gospel'. The remark is important.[11] For do we not often tend to define monastic life in terms of what is unique to it, in terms of regulations about monastic liturgy, ritual, clothing, fasting, and so forth? I do not say that these things are unimportant, but they are fundamentally *rubrics*, accidental expressions of essential values. And Christ categorically insisted that no amount of outward observance can substitute for an absence of inward truth. Our vow of obedience is above all a vow to obey Christ's commandments. 'Love the Lord God with all your heart.' 'Honour everyone.' 'Never do to another what you do not want done to yourself.' 'Visit the sick.' 'Console the sorrowing.' 'Do not repay a bad turn.' 'Love your enemies.'[12] If we do not obey *these* passages of the Rule and others like them, taken straight from the Gospel, it will profit us little if, at the last, we protest that we have never spoken a word after Compline.

The second axiom comes from Chapter 43: 'Let nothing be preferred to the Work of God.'[13] It touches on more than just our obligation to recite the Divine Office. It concerns the disposition of our heart. The monk is to make the Divine Office the centre of his life. He must not let any exterior engagement interfere with it. He is to cultivate a love of it that will define his existence. And why? Our *Constitutions* tell us. When the monastic community gathers for the Work of God, it 'fulfils Christ's priestly function, offering to God a sacrifice of praise and making intercession for the salvation of the whole world'.[14]

Just think of it: we who are gathered in this room, monks of Mount Saint Bernard, are entrusted with the enactment of Christ's priestly intercession, commissioned to pray constantly that the *kosmos* may find salvation. This noble service is one we perform together. In our community, our particular church, we are to manifest what the universal Church signifies globally: a world reconciled and made one.[15] By obeying this precept, by putting nothing before the Work of God, we assume our share in Christ's salvific work.

The third axiom calls for little comment. It comes from Chapter 57: 'That in all things God may be glorified.'[16] Every part of our life, of our day, has potential to become a liturgy of praise. Nothing is too small. 'Is this for the glory of God?' By letting that question test all our thoughts and words, our deeds, encounters and relationships, we shall be equipped with a sure standard of obedience. We shall have Christ, our true King, always before our eyes. And who would not want to follow him to glory?

Years ago I found the memoirs of Lucia dos Santos, one of the visionaries of Fatima, in our library. I decided to read it, and so discovered the account of a conversation Lucia had with Jacinta, another seer, at the time of the apparitions. Lucia had given the younger girl a picture of the Sacred Heart, an image she herself admired greatly. Jacinta, however, saw it differently. She exclaimed: 'It's so ugly! It doesn't look like Our Lord at all. He is so beautiful! But I want it; it is He just the same.'[17]

1. The three visionaries of Fatima, Jacinta on the right, visibly with a mind of her own.

With a child's wisdom she had arrived at a subtle insight into the theological nature of signs. She, who had beheld the glory of the Lord, instantly recognized the image as being repellently inadequate, yet received it gratefully because of the beauty of Him whom it represented. We find an analogous incident in the biography of Faustina Kowalska. When shown the first painted image of Divine Mercy, Faustina's response was as categorical as Jacinta's, though less abrupt. She was older, after all, and Polish. Yet she, too, came with time to accept that an imperfect image may, to eyes of faith, point to a perfect prototype.

I think it essential to bear this in mind when we reflect on obedience to superiors in a Benedictine community. The superior is believed, says Benedict, to 'represent Christ'.[18] It is a pill we may find hard to swallow. What if his temperament and sensibility are at loggerheads with ours? What if we cannot help thinking, whenever he opens his mouth: 'What does *he* know?' Can we claim to see in him an image of Christ? Yes, if we manage to make Jacinta's distinction. To profess that Christ acts in a personal way through our Superior is not to ascribe mystic perfection to someone whose imperfections may well cry out. It does not imply an ecclesial version of Andersen's tale of the emperor's new clothes. The profession we make speaks primarily, not of our Superior, but of Christ. It expresses our conviction that God's infallible providence operates through fallible human beings. That it really touches us in real circumstances. Monastic obedience is not arbitrary. Its terms are rigorously defined and, as such, blessed by the Church, which daringly presents it as an assured channel of grace.

This claim is so counter-intuitive that it needs to be unpacked. A helpful perspective can be found in a letter to the Order from Dom Gabriel Sortais during his term as abbot general (1951–63). 'Obedience', he wrote,

> is the *only reasonable position* to adopt for anyone who lives within a logic of faith. It is not a matter of approving what should not be approved. It is a matter of believing that Christ, by humanly deficient means, makes obedience carry blessings that exceed the designs of human wisdom. It is not the Superior we consider infallible, but Christ's action.[19]

The monastic tradition insists that obedience is a source of grace *ipso facto* because it is a response motivated by faith. It is not calculated or self-seeking. Never is our trust in Christ's omnipotence put more sorely to the test than when we have to invest it in the brittleness of human beings. Never is the spiritual reward, and the freedom it brings, greater than when we make the leap despite all, and find the 'everlasting arms' (cf. Deuteronomy 33.27) catching us in the midst of what seemed to be an abyss of free fall.

It is important, though, not to imagine the practice of obedience in unduly dramatic terms. The legislation of the Rule maintains it within bounds. The most absolute obedience is required of the superior himself. He is to observe the Rule 'in every particular'.[20] He is not to discredit by deeds what he upholds by word. He is to respond, with superhuman flexibility, to the temperaments, gifts and limitations of all his brethren. When asked to command, it is to safeguard objective observance, that is, to make sure, quite simply, that the monks keep their word.

Each of us has made a covenant with the Lord. The Rule is our contract. In solemn assembly we have begged to keep it for the rest of our lives. We entertain the certainty that no other way leads more directly to the end we long for: the vision of God on his holy mountain in a perfection of love free of fear. When St Benedict exhorts the superior to correct, and not to neglect, practice that compromises integral observance of the Rule, it is for the benefit of those who have professed it. Why waste money on food that does not satisfy? Why ramble in dark woods when the royal highway opens up before us? Cîteaux at its best has always had an enthusiasm for the Rule and unshakeable confidence in it. We might ask: have we?

St Benedict's superior, then, is not a lion preparing to spring, armed with random orders. More often than not, his admonitions will be gentle reminders to honour a commitment freely made. He will aim to breathe on the flame of our fidelity to make it burn more brightly, more beautifully, while never ceasing to implore the Lord to keep his own lamp from going out. Sometimes, yes, he will request individuals to accept structural change: a new job or a new way of doing things. His suggestions will be animated by concern for the common good. Nothing is more fatal than a superior pursuing a private design masqueraded as 'the will of God'.

A further aspect to the superior's ministry was brought home to me by something a wise abbot wrote to me shortly after I took office. 'The biggest burden of the abbatial office', I was told, 'is that you must call your Brothers to accept their cross, their share in the redemptive life of the Lord Jesus. To do that, you must know the Brothers and help them discern the mystery of Jesus in their lives.'[21]

How can one correspond to such a commission? St Benedict gives us a hint when he describes the kind of relationship that should obtain between monks and their superior. The superior, he says, is to love everyone with equal charity; the monks are to show him 'unfeigned love'. This may seem to bring us back to square one. What if we do not *like* our superior? What if the superior feels scant natural sympathy for some of his brethren? Should we find ourselves in this predicament, we must remind ourselves which star we are steering by.

A monastery is not a club. It is a supernatural reality. The relationships we enjoy within it, though imbued with human warmth, are supernatural. While 'love' to many of our contemporaries is a function of emotion, it points, in St Benedict vocabulary, to a more ancient definition. Here, to 'love' is to wish others well and to do well to them; to will to find them loveworthy; to see them in the light of God's love. That, by grace, we can do. It is an attitude of mind that over time can even transform the sentiment of the heart.

The bedrock of obedience, then, is determined goodwill exercised with resolute trust – on both sides, naturally. Finally, let us remember that personal obedience of this kind is not limited to our relationship with our superior. It should, St Benedict insists, inform all our relationships in community.[22] All the brethren are potential 'representatives of Christ'. It is a good exercise to look round, sometimes, in church or in chapter, to really *see* the brethren, to look at each one with charity and gratitude, and to remind oneself: 'This is the word of Christ to me.' Or even: 'This is the Christ I am called to serve.' Then even the dullest winter morning can suddenly be flooded with Tabor light.

STABILITY: TO ESTABLISH ROOTS

When Joshua, after four decades in the desert, led Israel into the Promised Land, it was by a process that mirror-imaged the exodus from Egypt. Once again waters parted and were gathered in a heap. Once again Israel walked dry-shod on land that had so far been touched only by water-creatures. The crossing of the Jordan concluded a chapter that had opened with the crossing of the Red Sea. That chapter had spelt an experience of acute homelessness. The homelessness had a pedagogical purpose. It was designed to make the people understand that their fundamental identity depended, not on geographical boundaries, but on observance of God-given laws. When the lesson seemed to have been assimilated, they were led back to Canaan in order, as the Psalm says, that *there* they might keep what they had learnt (Psalm 104.44f.).

While the Jordan towered over them, Joshua ordered 12 men to pass into the midst of the river 'and take up stones upon your shoulders according to the number of the tribes of Israel' (Joshua 4.5). Joshua had these stones placed in Gilgal, on the west bank. There they remained as a sign. Future generations would be bound to ask what they meant. And so their elders could retell the story of God's faithfulness. Gilgal was a sanctuary of remembrance, a memorial to mighty deeds. That is why it was an appropriate spot for the inauguration of Israel's kingdom, intended (in principle) to guarantee the covenant. That is why it was a double scandal when, in later centuries, Gilgal of all places became a centre of idolatry, torpedoed by the indictments of Amos and Hosea.

This one example from the fifteenth-century reconquest conveys a message proclaimed to us from the earliest pages of Scripture. It is a message of paradox. It asks us to keep together in our minds two essential principles that, to reason uninformed by revelation, might seem contradictory: on the one hand, we are told that Israel's God is a transcendent God who cannot be contained by anything in creation; on the other, we are told that this same God intervenes in particular circumstances and places, leaving his mark on our world and history. Our unknowably exalted God acts in knowable ways. He is a God who leaves traces.

We see him doing just that in the Garden of Eden, which remains the supreme symbol of an earthly sanctuary. But the radiance of God's presence on earth soon extended to other places, too, as salvation history progressed and people came to realize that God had 'made his home among men' (Revelation 21.3). When Abraham entered Palestine, he walked up and down the length of the land proclaiming, 'the Lord' (Genesis 12.8, 13.4, etc.), claiming it for him. Patriarchs and prophets followed suit, each according to his genius. Gilgal is but one of many places in which Israel commemorated encounters with the living God, certain that a force of divine visitation lingered in their earth and stones and very dust.

This attachment to holy places takes a gigantic forward leap during the reign of David. His destiny became inseparable from that of the city he made his own: Jerusalem, the vision of peace, city of David, city of God. Its name came to express the core of Israel's hope for temporal and eternal beatitude. Through the medium of the Psalms we, too, sing its praises daily. It is striking that St Benedict would have us begin each day with the Psalm David sang 'when he fled from Absalom his son' (Psalm 3),[23] making a hasty escape from Jerusalem, not knowing whether he would ever return. David, Scripture tells us, went barefoot, his head covered, weeping as he went (2 Samuel 15.30). But he sang. The monk is to let that same song set the tone for each day's worship. The thought of his exile is to kindle in him a spirit of repentance and longing. Only thus can he respond with just wonder as the day unfolds and he sees, carried on currents of psalmody, that the grace of God has, in fact, brought him, the wanderer, home.

For to the follower of Jesus, Jerusalem represents not merely a prospect for the end of time, when the Lord will gather him and all the faithful into the city where the Lamb will be their lamp 'and the sea will be no more' (Revelation 21.1). The gates of Jerusalem stand open to him here and now. Monks have always been certain of this, and nowhere, perhaps, do we find that certainty better expressed than in St Bernard's letter to Bishop Alexander of Lincoln, who rejoiced in the epithet, 'the Magnificent'. You remember the circumstances. Philip, a canon of Alexander's cathedral, had called in at Clairvaux on his way to Jerusalem and been so overwhelmed by the monastery, bursting with life, that he felt no need to continue his pilgrimage. He desired only to stay with what he had found. It is worth quoting Bernard at length as he explains to Alexander what had happened:

I write to tell you that your Philip has found a short cut to Jerusalem and has arrived there very quickly. He crossed 'the vast ocean stretching wide on every hand' with a favourable wind in a very short time, and he has now cast anchor on the shores for which he was making. Even now he stands in the courts of Jerusalem [...]. He has entered the holy city and has chosen his heritage with them of whom it has been deservedly said: 'You are no longer exiles and aliens; the saints are your fellow citizens, you belong to God's household.' His going and coming is in their company and he has become one of them, glorifying God and saying with them: 'We find our true home in heaven.'

He is no longer an inquisitive onlooker, but a devout inhabitant and an enrolled citizen of Jerusalem; but not of that earthly Jerusalem [...] which is in bondage with her children, but of the free Jerusalem which is above and the mother of us all. And this, if you want to know, is Clairvaux.[24]

There is more, here, than rhetorical flourish. In his inimitable way, Bernard gives voice to an insight that is well grounded. A real monastery *is* a Jerusalem: a holy place and a place of encounter. It is the setting of a solemn covenant where the monk promises to remain fully God's, and where God, in turn, promises to bestow himself. In the monastery, the monk steps inside sacred history. He is no longer content to admire it from a distance. Bernard spells this out: the monk 'is no longer an inquisitive onlooker, but an enrolled citizen of Jerusalem'. He has come home.

Bernard's estimation of Clairvaux can, and should, be transferred to our circumstances. Mount Saint Bernard: our Jerusalem! We can dare to make the connection without fear of presumption. This place is for us a sacrament of presence, a holy city, the gate of heaven. Here we have given God our lives, once for all; here God gives himself to us, continuously. This is an objective truth. It is the foundation of our stability, the bedrock of our fidelity. We have bound ourselves to this place because we trust that this is where our hopes will be fulfilled; this is where we are given what we need to serve, love and know the living God.

Our Jerusalem is one that needs to be constructed anew every day, obviously. We are at once its stones and its craftsmen. Yet eyes of faith can discern it as a sign of the eternal Jerusalem, already perfect and radiant in splendour. Our feet stand in its courts. Our stability keeps them from stumbling.

In addition to this symbolic, biblical significance, monastic stability has an aspect that is more pragmatic. For when the early monks began to practise *stabilitas loci* it was as a tool in the spiritual craft. It helped them, so they discovered, in the pursuit of their goal. What was that goal? They would have answered in various ways. Some would have said, 'knowledge of God'; others, 'observing the commandments'; others, 'union with Christ'. But all would have agreed that a basic trait of their quest was the dimension of the spirit they called *hesychia*. This Greek term is familiar to us from the word 'Hesychasm', which designates a mystical revival propagated from the late eighteenth century, whose influence was felt in every corner of Europe's Christian East. We may think that we dare not aspire to such heights. But *hesychia* is not a function of ecstatic spirituality. What it stands for is more humble and universal. It is enough to remember that the term comes into Latin as *Pax*, which has for centuries been the motto of Benedictines. We catch something of its flavour from an anonymous hymn come down to us in the sayings of the Desert Fathers:

O peace, pathway to the kingdom of heaven! [...]
O peace, that every day, every night, waits for Christ
and keeps the lamp burning, desiring Christ and

singing to him ceaselessly, 'My heart is ready, O God, my heart is ready!' [...] O peace, field of Christ bearing a lovely harvest![25]

To live in *hesychia*, to be a 'hesychast', is to live in a state of alert attention so that our whole being is attuned to the presence of Christ. It is a state we endeavour to reach so that we can remain entirely at the Lord's disposal. This kind of peace is no sweet slumber; it is not a matter of leaning back and waiting to see what will happen. Any such notion is put right by a saying attributed to Anthony the Great: 'He who sits alone in quiet [*hesychazōn*] has escaped from three wars: of hearing, speaking, and seeing; but there is one thing against which he must continually fight: that is, his own heart.'[26] The peace we find on removing ourselves from the din and distraction of the city, the peace of enclosure, is in the first instance a means to an end. It is peace imposed on noise from without in order that we might hear the noise within. Ascetic rest, then, is designed to reveal the heart's unrest. It is, in Anthony's phrase, a condition of spiritual warfare. What this amounts to in practice is evident from another *apophthegm* that it will be worth citing in full.

There were three friends, committed fellows, who became monks. One of them chose to make peace between men who were fighting, according to what is written, 'Blessed are the peacemakers'. The second chose to visit the sick. The third chose to go away and pursue *hesychia* in solitude. Now the first, having laboured on account of people's quarrels, could not sort them all out. Depressed, he went to him who looked after the sick, and found him, too, discouraged, unable to fulfil the commandment. They agreed, then, to go and see the hermit. They laid their affliction before him, then asked how he himself was getting on. He was silent for a while, then poured water into a vessel and said, 'Look closely at the water.' It was stirred up. A little later, he said again, 'Look now, how still the water has become.' And when they looked into the water they saw, as in a mirror, their own faces. Then he told them, 'This is how it is with anyone living in the midst of other people. On account of agitation, he does not see his sins; but when he enters *hesychia*, above all in solitude, then he sees his faults.'[27]

Here we have much food for thought. The first thing to note is that all three men were 'committed'. They were equally earnest in their will to follow Christ. The point of the story is *not* to drive a wedge between the 'active' and the 'contemplative' life.

We are asked, rather, to consider the spirit in which we put our neck to Christ's yoke and to recognize that even the noblest motivation must be purified. That is where the stillness of the desert is indispensable, as we learn from the third monk's physics experiment. When he first filled his bowl with water, it was full of particles. It revealed nothing. Only when the mud had settled did the water lend itself to the purpose for which it was intended. For what did the brothers see when they looked into it? They saw themselves, 'as in a mirror'. Before we can hope to see the face of Christ, before we can see our neighbour as he is, in love and truth, we must have the courage to be still and to look ourselves straight in the eyes. For that purpose, we practise stability. For that purpose, we value our enclosure.

We all know Abba Moses' saying: 'Remain in your cell, it will teach you everything.'[28] The principle is timeless. We have come to the school of the Lord's service to learn. We shall acquire no wisdom if we skive lessons. If we are serious about our contemplative purpose, we must constantly renew our commitment to the cell, to the enclosure, to outward and inward stability. We know it is not always easy. The Fathers acknowledged that it is possible for the mind to be cavorting in Alexandria even while the body stays put in the monastic settlement of Scetis.

Our stability now is more at risk than it has ever been before. In addition to the perennial temptations of monks, we are exposed to virtual and visual media. They potentially make us waste massive amounts of time. Worse still, they can distract our minds and hearts, hindering the unification and pacification we came to the monastery to seek. How easy it is to be caught up in vicious circles.

The more I depend on distraction, the harder it is to recollect myself in prayer and stillness. As a result, I depend on distractions even more, to fill my days and nights with *something*. Instead of settling, the water in my bowl becomes ever murkier. In one of his sermons on the Song of Songs, the twelfth-century Cistercian Gilbert of Hoyland gives us a wonderful incentive to renew our commitment to stability in enclosure. The enclosure, says he, is the garden where the Lord awaits us, a place of sweet encounter to which we are privileged to be admitted:

If it is your desire to offer your heart to Christ as a garden of delights, do not take it ill if you are enclosed by this rampart [*viz.* the strictness of the Rule]. Anyone who murmurs in secret on account of this bulwark, wishes in fact to lose delights that are his, if indeed he does possess them. One who does not know how to be enclosed, does not know how to be a garden.[29]

Such a one remains uncultivated wilderness, 'a solitude' in the language of the Old Testament. For enclosure, says Gilbert, means encounter. It is Love itself.

In the *Exordium Parvum*, a key source of the founding of our Order, we find a brief but telling portrayal of Alberic, the second abbot of Cîteaux. Bereft of its first pastor, recalled to Molesme, 'the church of Cîteaux gathered, and by regular election raised up a brother named Alberic to be their abbot. He was a man of learning, well versed in studies both divine and human, a lover of the Rule and of the brethren.'[30] It is worth noting the reference to the community as 'church': *cisterciensis ecclesia*. It tells us something about the self-understanding of Cîteaux.

The monastic community is not an assembly of mere individuals pursuing similar goals, drawn and held together by considerations of utility. The community is a communion, a body with many members. It is a microcosmic reflection of the Church, the mystic spouse of Christ, which, for extending to east and west, north and south, yet maintains one heart, one soul. It is fitting that Alberic, a man both learned and wise, should stand before us with a strong attachment, not only to the place and rule, but to the brethren. The monastic life cannot be conceived of or lived in abstract terms. It involves full and definitive insertion into a human reality, with all the joys and challenges such experience brings. I should like to say a few words about this dimension of our stability.

What is the role of the community in our lives of monastic *conversatio*? The tradition stresses two aspects. Let us first consider the more austere. The community constitutes a constant test of our integrity. From the way in which we interact with our brethren, we see whether we are in fact growing in conformity to Christ or whether progress is only apparent in the protective solitude of our cell, with the door locked from the inside. Some monastic Fathers were virulent in their polemic against hermits. How can people who live alone, they asked, pretend to live fully Christian lives in the absence of companions on whom to exercise their patience, endurance, mercy and charity?

Above all, the Fathers regarded the community as a school of humility. If you recall the seventh chapter of the Rule, you will find that every step of St Benedict's Ladder of Humility (and no other way reaches the heights to which we aspire) is a function of interpersonal relationships. The brethren exercise us, in every sense of the word. For that we should be grateful, even when we are caused to suffer. Life in common forces us every day to purify our heart and mind. We are taught what it means to 'walk by faith, not by sight'. This is especially so when we find ourselves in situations of conflict that seem to defy human resolution.

In his *Practical and Theological Chapters*, St Simeon the New Theologian speaks of the fruit to be reaped at such times:

If a man habitually loves and prays for those who injure and treat him unjustly, those who hate him and shun his presence, he will make great progress in a short time. For when we feel this in our hearts, it plunges all our thoughts into the abyss of humility.[31]

Let me state the obvious: this is a monk talking to monks! Simeon knew that monastic life is not always a bed of roses. He does not fob us off with facile promises. But note that he does not say, 'Grin and bear it.' Nor does he say, 'Poor you!' He calls on us, rather, to enter 'the abyss of humility'.

Why? Because it is there, in the place of most urgent need, where we have no illusions about our own strength, that we encounter Christ as a living presence, as our Redeemer. We have embarked on a serious, indeed a dangerous quest. To see Christ 'as he is', we have to see ourselves 'as we are', dust from dust, sinners in need of salvation, men of boundless poverty. Our stability in community helps us reach this insight. It would be unbearable, were it not for the fact that it is there, *in* the depths, that God's mercy embraces us, makes us new, and turns our grief into joy and praise. Have we the courage to enter the place where our Saviour awaits us?

Of course, this is not all. The character of the monastic community as a battlefield is complemented by another dimension no less fundamental. It is wonderfully summarized in a verse from Ecclesiastes that our Cistercian Fathers loved to repeat: 'Woe to him who is alone, for he has no one to raise him up when he falls!' (4.10). The Lord's call has brought us together in this community, this church of ours, to help, sustain, and encourage one another. On the day of our profession, we made a commitment not only to a plot of land, but to a community of brethren. We pledged ourselves to give them our best and to help them in any way we can; they, by admitting us, pledged the same. Indeed, their pledge preceded ours. They promised to show us the 'mercy' we asked for at our clothing, and to continue showing it for as long as we journey together.

The Rule refers to monks in community as brothers. That is how we address and think of one another. It is not a vain word. To have a brother is to enter a relation that goes deeper even than friendship. It is to find our place within a permanent, enduring reality that carries us, even as we are called to carry our brethren. Dear Brother Gabriel was fond of citing Proverbs (18.19, in the Septuagint version): 'A brother helped by a brother is a strong city.' Through a monastic life lived faithfully, wholeheartedly for seven decades, he had learnt how true it is.

It is essential that we do not lose sight of that last dimension of beatitude. Yes, the common life can be a trial. It stretches us and forces us to grow, even when we prefer to vegetate in more or less complacent indolence. But life in community is also joy. The monastic life flourishes best at times and in places where the brethren are able to delight in being together, thankful for the grace of vocation that unites them in building a living temple for the Lord of lords. St Bernard, who can often seem rather forbidding, even harsh, becomes lyrical when he speaks of his love of the community. He was able, his biographers tell us, to create, at Clairvaux, an environment in which the Psalmist's words were fulfilled, where the dew of Hermon and a sweet-smelling oil like Aaron's made the experience of fraternal life in common delightful.

Were we to do the rounds of other centres of twelfth-century monasticism, we should find the same aspiration and a firm resolve to make it come true. The same challenge is ours today. The Lord, who has brought us together, invites us to create unity out of constituent elements that are, I think it is true to say, wonderfully diverse. St Benedict tells us how we go about the work of construction. If we list the key words by which he legislates for fraternal relationships, we end up with an inspiring charter: 'encourage one another'; 'harbour neither jealousy nor hatred of anyone'; 'outdo one another in showing honour'. Look at your brethren with 'reverence', he tells us: 'obey' them and 'console' them when they are sad.[32] It is with tools such as these that we construct our strong city, the stable setting of our ceaseless conversion.

Monastic stability has a temporal as well as a spatial aspect. By our vow of stability we promise not only to remain in a given place, faithful to a given group of people; we commit ourselves to a given rhythm of life. We undertake to regulate our days in a defined way. St Benedict exhorts us time and again to remain faithful to the horarium. Why? The first, most pragmatic reason concerns what we might call the concentration of spiritual energy. It is a perspective congenial to us moderns, living as we do in energy-conscious times. We endeavour to maximize the productivity of power and not to squander it. A monastery *is* a powerhouse. It is something visitors, even those unfamiliar with our life, often remark on. What they notice is, I think, the vigour

49

that ensues when a community of men unites in a shared purpose. An indefinable quality of lightness, of sparkle, results where a common enterprise is pursued with unity of intention. The community acquires a strength that exceeds the sum of individual contributions; we find ourselves carried through tasks and challenges that looked set to weigh us down.

It is unsurprising that movements of monastic renewal have almost invariably begun by eliminating idiorhythmicity, that is, the tendency of monks to organize their personal timetables on subjective criteria, apart from the movement of the community. The rebirth of Athonite monasticism in the second half of the last century is a case in point. One by one the idiorhythmic monasteries and lavras of Athos returned to a common discipline and common life. Thereby, stumps widely thought to be past flourishing produced not only new branches, but fruit in plenty.

Our own tradition is rich in similar examples. We need only think of Port Royal under the abbacy of Angélique Arnauld in the first half of the seventeenth century. Within a decade, the rediscovery of cenobitic observance turned what was effectively a hostel for spinsters of means into a contagiously fervent community.

If we imagine the monastery as a generator, we have two options: to feed it or to tap it. We feed it by whole-hearted participation and regularity, by determinedly placing our common work before personal projects. We tap it by opting out and going our own way. The energy and joyfulness of our house depend on the choices each one of us makes daily.

A second aspect of temporal stability resides in the opportunity it gives us to reaffirm priorities. We know from both experience and revelation that 'where our treasure is, there our hearts will be also' (Matthew 6.21). We live in a world where time is money. The way we use time reveals a lot, to ourselves and to others, about what matters to us. The horarium indicated by the Rule, defined by our *Constitutions* and *Customary*, intends to make the treasure of time an offering to God, a sacrifice of praise that lifts hearts up instead of tying them down. The bells that govern our lives recall us, day and night, to essentials. They invite us to recover the orientation of our hearts, should they have been distracted.

As soon as the bell for Office goes, says St Benedict, monks should drop whatever occupies them and hasten to church. This haste, exercised with due gravity, is not primarily motivated by a fear of being late. We make haste, rather, to train ourselves in putting first things first. The Benedictine subconscious is haunted by the image of the monastic scribe who leaves a lovely Gothic capital unfinished on hearing the first bell for Vespers.[33] We know what sacrifice is sometimes required in tearing ourselves away from tasks that have absorbed our attention and given us pleasure. We also know how our will, stubborn as it is, is gradually moulded by such ascesis, becoming prompter and more responsive.

Nor should we underestimate the impact of our regularity on others, as a testimony to supernatural values. There is a pertinent passage in David Knowles's memoir of Abbot Butler in which he describes how the brethren at Downside knew

that whatever the matter under discussion (short of the rarest extremity) the abbot would break off to make his half-hour's prayer before supper; they also knew that at the sound of the bell for Office he would immediately rise; and all this served as a most salutary tonic.[34]

Note Knowles's choice of metaphor. A single man's commitment to prayer served to invigorate and buoy an entire community. Far from turning us into shackled sleepwalkers, resolute regularity forms the will and frees it, bestowing vitality within and around us. It is a tonic we can pour each other every day. It is perhaps the most effective form of fraternal encouragement. By rooting ourselves ever anew in our first, dearest love, and by expressing that love in acts, our hearts' stability gives sense to the stability of our bodies.

This, surely, is the crux of the matter: a third aspect of regularity that sums up the first two. What to outsiders can look like busyness – days broken up into fragments, where we rarely perform a single activity for more than a couple of hours at a time – is a tool by which we hope to attain *hesychia*, the *pax* towards which monastic discipline is directed. We have seen that stability in the cell is designed to bring out the heart's unrest, so that it can be dealt with and submitted to divine grace. Temporal stability has a similar purpose. It presents a constant challenge to self-will, which always attempts to assert itself against regular discipline. The bell is often enough a call to battle, to the battle of the heart that Anthony singled out as the monk's primary occupation.

And so we find, yet again, that our vow of stability constitutes an enduring test of purpose. St Bernard used to ask himself throughout his novitiate, 'Bernard,

Bernard why have you come?'[35] Our practice of stability, not only for a year or two but for life, requires us to make that question our own and to supplement it with one even more challenging: 'Why do you remain?' Should we find we hesitate in giving an answer, every day offers countless opportunities to make amends and to renew good zeal. We have only to 'follow the flock', in that phrase from the Song of Songs (1.8) our Fathers loved to cite in season and out of season.

And we can be sure of this: in the monastery, this promised land of ours, this blessed garden to which, by no merit of our own, we have been called, God's faithfulness infallibly precedes ours. If we maintain the will to keep what we have promised, his love will carry us to heights beyond our reach. We shall find rest in our labour, and gladness. We shall build up our community in a communion of love, finding strength and sustenance in one another. And the Lord will be our portion.

CONVERSATIO MORUM: TO KEEP GROWING

The time has come to say something about our third vow, that of *conversatio morum*. It may be useful to begin by exploring its resonance in Scripture. The literal meaning of 'conversion' is, of course, 'a turning round'. It is well to keep that definition in mind when we look for 'conversion' in the Bible, for then we are dealing with trends and patterns rather than straightforward literal occurrences. In fact, if you look 'conversion' up in a concordance of the *New Revised Standard Version* of the Bible, you will see that the word is used only once, in Acts 15.3, when St Paul reports to the apostles about the '*epistrofē* of the Gentiles'. Like the Latin '*conversio*', '*epistrofē*' has a primary sense that is spatial. It denotes a turning round as change of direction. As for the personal noun 'convert', the *NRSV* uses it three times: in Matthew 23.15, to render '*prosēlutos*', meaning a novice Pharisee; in Romans 16.5, to paraphrase St Paul's description of his friend Epaenetus as 'a firstfruit for Christ'; and in 1 Timothy 3.6, to translate '*neophytos*' – that is, someone who has newly emerged from the waters of baptism.

This list of examples shows us that Christian 'conversion' is not reducible to a single reality or experience. For being a familiar word, it remains elusive. Like most metaphors, it is capable of sustaining a variety of meanings, depending on the imagination and associations of individuals. To unravel some of them, we can usefully conduct an enquiry into images of 'turning round' in the Bible. By this means we shall be able to trace the emergence of 'conversion' as a theological term and get some idea of the reality it sought to encapsulate.

The call to 'turn' resonates forcefully throughout the Scriptures. Men and women are created to live before God as his servants and friends, in unselfconscious enjoyment of his presence. Yet the power of sin, whose hallmark is an urge to break away, drives them from their true purpose in tragic imitation of their forebears who, after eating the forbidden fruit, 'hid themselves from the presence of the Lord God' (Genesis 3.8). The 'return' the Bible speaks of answers an invitation from the God who, once and for all, has set his people as a seal upon his heart, with a love strong as death.

The motif of return is also an expression of fallen man's nostalgia for Eden. In his heart of hearts, he hears conflicting voices: one that urges him to scale the garden walls and follow his own ways; another that draws him back to his origins, away from the isolating chaos of his corrupted will to the ordered calm of Paradise, which is inhabited by things and beings he can name, and therefore relate to in communion. The history of salvation is the story of wayward sinners who long to return to the Garden, to the Promised Land, to Jerusalem. Their 'conversion' is a turning round to appropriate their origins in God, by rejecting sin's false promises and by letting their personal will be conformed to the will of God. The process will be complete when there is no longer a need to keep turning; when their lives have become a straight path focused sharply on God, like that of the four living creatures seen by Ezekiel in the fifth year of King Jehoiachin's exile. Untouched by Adam's rebellion, those angelic beings 'moved straight ahead, without turning as they moved' (1.12). They were fixed on, drawn towards, and governed by 'the appearance of the likeness of the glory of God' (1.28).

'Turning round' can be a risky business. It confronts us with ourselves, with our past, with missed opportunities. Sometimes we lose our bearings and end up getting dizzy walking round ourselves. Think of the Israelites in the desert, after the exodus. They knew they had to leave captivity: there was no problem about that. But it took them 40 years of walking round and round before they were ready to enter the Promised Land. 'Conversion' takes time. It requires a purification of the will and a readiness to leave familiar, signposted paths. 'My ways are not your ways', said the Lord to Isaiah (55.8f.).

Again and again, the Bible recounts how individuals make that experience for themselves by being led into the wilderness, which is an uncomfortable, scary, lonely place, but also a place of freedom. Away from the clutter of human dwellings, the desert affords visitors an opportunity to gain new perspectives, to contemplate the horizon. It is in the wilderness that God's people learn what they are being converted *to*.

To ancient Israel, the principal tool of conversion was the Law. The Mosaic code constituted a list of commandments of divine origin: the tablets of the covenant were 'the work of God, and the writing was the writing of God' (Exodus 32.16). Our modern minds, accustomed to post-Reformation expositions of Pauline rhetoric, sometimes forget what a blessing the Law was to Israel. 'What other great nation', says Moses to the people in the desert, 'has a god so near to it as the Lord our God is whenever we call to him? And what other great nation has statutes and ordinances as just as the entire law that I am setting before you today?' (Deuteronomy 4.7–8). The Law was a pledge of God's favour. By keeping it, the Israelites were assured of one day entering the land God had promised them, where he would live among them. The injunctions of the Mosaic code are both moral and cultic. This complementarity corresponds to the dual focus of Israel's 'conversion'. It was both ethical and geographical: focused on the presence of God's will in his Law and on his mystical presence in the temple in Jerusalem.

During and after Israel's sojourn in Babylon, geography was increasingly subsumed into theological ethics. Trapped in the diaspora, the Jewish people could no longer realistically hope to return to the Holy Land. Thus the language of expulsion and return was translated into an idiom of trespass and repentance, with 'turning round' coming to mean a renewed commitment to practise the Law. When in their songs of lament the exiles vowed not to forget Jerusalem, they certainly had the actual city in mind. But Jerusalem, the city of God, was also becoming a symbol for a state of being in God's presence. The process can be followed in the cadences of the prophecy of Ezekiel, which ends with the words: 'And the name of the city from that time on shall be, The Lord is There' (48.35). The city of God is no longer primarily a location on the map. It is a sacrament of God's presence. To most exiled Jews who read the prophetic books in Asia Minor, North Africa or Europe, 'conversion' to that presence was accomplished through observance of the Law.

That mind-set was characteristic of the contemporaries of Jesus. Throughout his public ministry, Christ addressed, challenged and subverted it. As Western moderns, heirs to 20 centuries of Christian thought, we have a hard time appreciating the radicalism of some of Jesus' statements, by which he claimed to incarnate, in his person, the real object of Israel's religious hopes. In equating his body with the temple in Jerusalem, Jesus announced that centuries of cultic worship would find fulfilment in his resurrection from the dead. In claiming to fulfil the Law and the prophets, he implied that, in him, the mystery of Emmanuel was a palpable reality. 'Come to me', said Jesus, 'all you that are weary and carrying heavy burdens' (Matthew 11.28); 'Come, you that are blessed of my Father, inherit the kingdom' (Matthew 25.34); 'Come and see' where I abide (cf. John 1.39). From the moment of the Angel's annunciation to Mary, biblical 'conversion' acquires a new focus.

The 'turning round' in question is no longer directed towards gardens and cities and holy laws, but towards the person of Jesus.

2. Ezekiel's living creatures tamed and turned towards Christ. To move towards him is now what it means to proceed 'straight ahead'. From a thirteenth-century illumination.

The most remarkable 'conversion' story in the New Testament, whose significance is paradigmatic, is told when Jesus confronts the illness and death of Lazarus, his friend whom he 'loved'. Jesus' initial reaction, on being told that Lazarus was ill, is surprising. Both his disciples and Lazarus's family expect him to act; to go to his friend and console, even heal, him. But Jesus bides his time, assuring his followers that the illness will not lead to death, but is rather for God's glory, 'so that the Son of God may be glorified through it' (John 11.4). Forty-eight hours later Martha and Mary meet him with reproaches, convinced that 'if you had been here, [our] brother would not have died'. Jesus answers: 'Your brother will rise again', then adds, 'I am the resurrection' (11.21ff.). When he asks for Lazarus's tomb to be opened, Martha is horror-struck. She reminds him that 'there is already a stench'. Yet Jesus is adamant: 'Did I not tell you that if you believed, you would see the glory of God?' (11.39ff.)

He thus repeats the promise made to his disciples a few days before. Standing before the open grave, he commands Lazarus: 'Come out!' And the dead man *does* 'turn round', abandoning darkness and corruption, walking resolutely towards light and life in Jesus. 'Unbind him,' Jesus says, pointing to the burial cloths that recall the dominion of death, 'and let him go' (11.44). He then sets out on his final journey to Jerusalem, where he knows he himself will be put to death and laid in a tomb before rising again.

The story of Lazarus's raising represents all Christian conversion. Christ's summons to his dead friend is addressed to each one of us. St Paul universalizes it through the hymn he cites to the Christians at Ephesus: 'Sleeper awake! Rise from the dead, and Christ will shine upon you' (5.14). Christians are invited to turn away from the 'reign of death', which, from Adam, has kept mankind captive. They are instead to 'enter life', to pass from 'darkness' to 'light'. They are, that is, to turn towards Jesus, who *is* life and light. Paul knew the implications of such conversion from experience. The call of Jesus had made him turn round so completely that he ended up following the Way he had once sought to eliminate.

We have seen that Christian 'conversion' is a movement towards Jesus. It is also a movement into Jesus, as Paul kept declaring throughout his career: 'You have died, and your life is hidden with Christ in God' (Colossians 3.3); 'As many of you as were baptized have clothed yourselves with Christ' (Galatians 3.27). By virtue of baptism, their sacramental incorporation into the risen body of Christ, believers exist in union with him: their 'conversion' is already effected in so far as they are turned in the right direction, set on the path to follow. It is only brought to fulfilment, however, if they also let themselves be transformed by him. In the Fourth Gospel, Jesus says to his disciples: 'Abide in me as I abide in you' (John 15.4). The end of Christian conversion is for that mutual indwelling to become incarnate reality through the Holy Spirit. Christian converts should aspire to say that 'for me, living is Christ' (Philippians 1.21); that 'it is no longer I who live, but Christ who lives in me' (Galatians 2.20). At that point, their 'turning round' will be complete. They will have overcome the Adamic impulse to break away and 'hide' from God. They will be turned towards him with their whole being. They will 'see him as he is' (1 John 3.2) and be changed into his image, 'from one degree of glory to another' (2 Corinthians 3.18).

To be converted, then, is to turn towards God: to do his will and to strive to live in his presence. As such, it is a process with ethical implications. It requires us to abandon any behaviour that separates us from God. More essentially, however, 'conversion' is about surrendering to a force of attraction by being drawn into and conformed to divine life. 'Conversion' is prompted by God's initiative. It is pursued through a single-minded perseverance that engages and informs the will. It reaches fulfilment in a transformative union that is entirely the work of grace. It is a journey into God, restoring us to the purpose for which we were created in love. We have promised to keep travelling that road until our last breath.

I have outlined a biblical theology of conversion by way of commenting on our third Benedictine vow of *conversatio morum*. Some of you may be getting impatient. For if you look up 'conversatio' in a Latin dictionary, you find it does *not* mean 'conversion' but something quite different. Have I not got myself into a muddle? We should be addressing the question. After all, we have promised to exercise *conversatio morum* for the rest of our lives. It is as well to know what it really stands for.

The first thing to note is this: the reading '*conversatio morum*' in Chapter 58 of the Rule, legislating for monastic vows, was restored only quite recently. Until Abbot Butler published his critical edition of the Holy Rule just over a hundred years ago, the phrase in question read '*conversio morum*' in all current versions. From the ninth century, scribes had been correcting '*conversatio*' to '*conversio*' because the latter word made more sense.

It was only by assiduous recourse to ancient manuscripts that Butler summoned the courage to change this canonical reading back to '*conversatio*', which clearly was the notion of Benedict's choice. Let us take heart from this misreading of a thousand years' duration. It is not only we twenty-first-century monks, largely innocent of classical culture, who have trouble making sense of *conversatio morum*. Our medieval forebears, steeped in Latin literature, likewise struggled.

The noun '*conversatio*' derives from the verb '*conversari*', meaning 'to abide' or 'live with'. It acquired the general sense 'way of life'. The noun occurs several times in the Latin Bible used by St Benedict, notably in the letter to the Philippians, where the Vulgate has, '*nostra autem conversatio in caelis est*'. The *Revised Standard Version* translates this, 'our *commonwealth* is in heaven'. The notion '*conversatio*' thus points both to a manner of living and to the context in which that life is lived. In monastic literature '*conversatio monachorum*' came to mean 'monastic life'. In fact, the association of terms became so established that the specification '*monachorum*' was deemed redundant. We find a modern parallel to this development in the way in which we use the word 'religious' to designate a man or woman who has made religious *vows*, while an uninformed reader would assume that the term designates, more broadly, 'someone who believes in God'.

So far, so good. We can agree that '*conversatio*' means the 'way of life of monks', 'monastic behaviour'. But what about '*conversatio morum*'? The plural noun '*mores*' ('*morum*' in the genitive) stands for 'conduct'. Neither part of the composite is hard to translate. But their combination seems nonsensical. 'The way of life of conduct'? What might it mean to promise *that*? Fortunately, grammarians come to our assistance. In Low Latin, which is what Benedict wrote, it was common for two synonyms to be placed together in a genitive construction in order, quite simply, to establish a close link between them. In translating such phrases, we should put a conjunction like 'and' or 'or' instead of the genitive particle 'of'. If we supplement this conclusion with the point made earlier, that the adjective 'monastic' is implicit in St Benedict's phrase, we can translate *conversatio morum* along the lines of: 'a monastic way of life, that is to say, monastic behaviour'.

Abbot Butler, who recovered this phrase, sweated over it. Being a textual scholar, he refused to settle for compromises, and eventually declared *conversatio morum* to be untranslatable. His successor at Downside, Abbot Chapman, suggested 'monasticity', which for understandable reasons never caught on. Abbot McCann of Ampleforth plunged for the generous paraphrase 'self-discipline'. I suspect no definitive translation will ever be found. We may have to accept that we cannot quite render *conversatio morum*, while hoping that we agree on what it means.

Do we? This is where my earlier exposition of 'conversion' comes in. For if at profession we promise to observe 'a monastic way of life, monastic behaviour', it is obviously by contrast to *another* mode of conduct, which is that of the world. To be positively monastic is to negate something else; it is to be unworldly; to have turned round from what we used to be. The stakes are set out in St Benedict's Prologue. We monks, says Benedict, have given up everything to turn 'back to him from whom [we] had drifted through the sloth of disobedience'. We wish to leave the quagmire of self-will, pulling ourselves out by the strong cords of obedience.

And why? Because the focus of our life is no longer self but Christ. We desire one thing only: 'to follow him to glory'. Our monastic '*conversatio*' is a function of our conversion. It is the totality of means by which we keep ourselves turned round and on track until, like the cherubim, we have been so conformed to Christ that we move straight ahead without backsliding, running along the path of life with wills freed, hearts enlarged.

Monks must always be Christians *first*. It is our devotion to Christ, nothing else, that invests our monastic life with sense. *Conversatio morum*, far from being a matter of rituals, practices and observances, is the pact we make to belong to Christ and cling to him, preferring nothing to him. Of course there are rituals, practices and observances to keep, but we must always remember what these are for. They are means to an end. Without its living core, Christ himself, our regular life is an empty shell, we ourselves are but a travesty. We must keep our eyes fixed on the pillar of fire, ensuring that it is the Lord we follow, not our fancy.

For even monastic '*conversatio*' can become a servant of self-will. It is only too easy to regard it as something earned, something we keep as a possession or an insurance policy. If we yield to this mind-set, we shall, instead of opening up to grace, shut ourselves off from it. We shall be like a mussel whose pearl is destined to decay unseen in the depth of the sea. The true disciple of Jesus shuns securities. He moves determinedly into ever greater vulnerability. The less he relies on himself, the more he seeks to cast off his armour of defences, desiring to put on Christ only, and Christ crucified.

Our vow of *conversatio morum* is supposed to help us advance along this path of abandonment. If instead it wraps us up in protective clothing, it is an encumbrance, a hindrance, not a help.

Monastic history speaks again and again of monks and nuns who suddenly, after years in the habit, seem to wake up to what it is they are about. They then begin to live their lives with new conviction and radicalism. I am not speaking of the decadent and neglectful. I refer to people of virtuous, faithful, even admired lives. Think of Father Zosima in the *Life of Mary of Egypt*; think of St Stephen Harding; think of St Teresa at 40. They had all practised monastic *conversatio* faithfully from childhood, yet in each case we discern a definite before and after, a decisive moment at which their lives seem to combust, to remain thereafter a living flame. It is the moment in which their oblation is fully owned. Christ takes possession of them, and they hand themselves over to him unconditionally, recklessly, with utter trust. Not for nothing do they speak of that moment as their 'conversion'. That grace of theirs could be ours if we pray for it, and live up to what we pray for.

But how can we, through long years of monastic life, maintain a sufficient momentum of conversion? How can we ensure that our *conversatio morum* remains a fast-flowing, life-giving stream and does not turn into a stagnant pool full of pondweed? The Rule recommends four complementary practices that correspond to different dimensions of our nature.

The first of these we may call intellectual, inasmuch as it incites us to awareness, asking us to think about how we live. 'Harden not your hearts *today*' (Psalm 94.8). That solemn exhortation should permeate our consciousness day in, day out. St Benedict would have us sing it at Vigils every morning from the day we enter monastic life until the day we die.[36] 'The voice of the Lord calling us' is a feature not only of our initial vocation. It defines our whole life, forever calling us to new things. We must be vigilant, therefore, listen carefully, and reflect on what we hear, to act responsibly on what is asked of us. Fiery enthusiasm may mark our initial steps on the monastic path. As that path winds its way on and up, however, climbing steeply, something solider than zest is required for sustenance. We need to walk with understanding, with the serene strength of conviction.

The second practice proposed by St Benedict pertains to our moral lives. Here, too, he urges us to forge ahead. On leaving the world, we all experienced some degree of rupture as we abandoned habits unconducive to gospel living. These were not necessarily sinful, but they constituted distractions, dissipating energies we desired to unify in our pursuit of the one thing necessary. This initial change of lifestyle may have been demanding. We may look back on it with satisfaction, feeling as though, then, we accomplished something for God. So we did, I suppose, but only by way of making a start. The process of frank self-examination and courageous change must begin afresh continually.

St Benedict is aware of the *new* temptations and distractions we meet in the monastery. They are all the more insidious for being somewhat subtler. How prone we are to stash up reserves for rainy days under our mattress;[37] to think we deserve honour and privilege on account of our background, our seniority, our priesthood;[38] to compensate for monastic austerities by enjoying creature comforts on trips out.[39] Traps like these are as real today as in the sixth century. If we fall into them and, instead of breaking loose, make a comfortable nest for ourselves, we are in trouble. There is, then, a healthy unease we should cultivate, examining ourselves on basic points of observance and having the courage to see where we fail. God knows how easily we deceive ourselves.

The third aid to conversion presented in the Rule is of a spiritual nature. It is contained in a commandment we should bind for a sign upon our hand and carry as a frontlet between our eyes: 'prefer nothing to the love of Christ'.[40] We entered the monastery because Christ drew us; we wanted to serve, know and love him; we wanted to live on intimate terms with him. How essential it is to keep that first fascination alive, breathing on the flame of our fidelity. What is the 'contemplative' dimension of our life if not a deepening friendship with Christ? This friendship is also at the heart of our apostolate. It is 'in Christ' that we bear the joys and sorrows of our world before our Father in prayer.

And we are called to bear witness to the reality of Christ's love, showing that it is effective and transforming, able to fill a human life entirely, bearing fruit in charity, peace and joy. Pope Francis recently insisted on the 'prophetic' character of religious life. His challenge is as relevant to our life of enclosure as it is to Sisters of Mother Teresa working in inner cities: 'In the Church, religious are particularly called to be prophets.

They are called to bear witness to the way Jesus lived on this earth and to proclaim what the kingdom of God will be like in its perfection. A religious must *never* give up on prophecy.'[41] In essence, this is but a paraphrase of a passage from the First Letter of John. Its force derives from its being addressed specifically to us. Our role in the Church is to reveal the kingdom of heaven; to show others, by our lives, who Jesus is. It did not occur to St Benedict to articulate our calling in those terms, but he would certainly have approved of them. The Rule is a guide for becoming Christlike.

This brings us to the fourth way in which the Rule stimulates ongoing conversion. Let us call it 'ascetic'. It is an adjective that points to ways of getting and staying fit. St Benedict gives us a number of exercises to perform to keep our appetites in check. He tells us to use discernment in the way we eat, drink, sleep and cope with the body's instinctive desire for pleasure. Any first-time reader who expects the Rule to be a list of mortifications will, though, put it down with a sigh of dismay. It is not that St Benedict spurned specific practices or deemed them unimportant. Monks with the right attitude and aptitude can find all the guidance they need in his list of further reading in Chapter 73. But the asceticism he explicitly legislates for, making it binding on all, is different. It is relational.

In fact, it is fascinating to see how profoundly cenobitic the Rule is in all its aspects. The common life is everywhere the touchstone of authenticity. It is by assiduous practice in community life that the Benedictine monk is formed – formed and converted, turned round. What the Rule does at every juncture, even when dealing with quotidian matters, is this: it devises innumerable little tests to try our hearts, to reveal whether we have even begun to 'put on Christ', whether we are in fact, not just in principle, humble, charitable and obedient, whether we live by the Beatitudes. Remember, monastic life is supposed to be different. Other people expect us to learn something in the school of the Lord's service. We should expect it of ourselves. The extent of our conversion, the effectiveness of our *'conversatio'*, will show in the integrity of our *conversation*, in the root sense of that term, which indicates 'living among'. Here, each day presents new, salutary trials.

So *conversatio morum* is a supremely dynamic reality. It represents a resolve to reject complacency, to keep moving, never to become too comfortable. There are always new goals to reach. With the ardour of committed explorers, we have decided, once for all, to keep pressing on into the unknown. Thus we discover a creative, dialectic tension at the heart of our monastic profession. By our promise of stability we vow never to abandon a setting in which we remain in constant movement, impelled by obedience to Christ and his commandments, with the Rule as our guide. '*Caritas Christi urget nos*,' says St Paul in Jerome's rendering (2 Corinthians 5.14). The love of Christ impels and attracts us. It is always new, always greater. Happy are we who are called to know it and to make it known.

2

PATRIMONY

FLIGHT FROM THE WORLD

From the *Exordium Magnum*, that great account of our Order's beginnings, we are familiar with Br Laurence of Clairvaux who, shortly after the death of St Bernard, drove a herd of buffalo up through the length of Europe, from southern Italy to Burgundy.[42] It is a story that illustrates the unclassifiable richness of Cistercian vocations and the versatility of monks. Still, we might ask: what was Laurence, a monk of the abbey that was the flagship of Cistercian purity, doing gallivanting around the Mediterranean picking up exotic cattle? He was acting as legate of the community's prior, Dom Philip, who had business to transact with the king of Sicily.

This mission was not all that exceptional. Many early luminaries of the Order had a wide range of acquaintances and concomitant responsibilities. The monks of Clairvaux looked back, of course, to the example of their founding abbot. Called upon to help in the most varied circumstances, St Bernard responded generously. Some of his most intimately contemplative sermons were preached between exhausting bouts of continental travel. He referred to himself plaintively as the 'chimera of the age',[43] conscious of the contradictions his life seemed to display.

Looking further afield, we find other Cistercians, too, maintaining an impressive range of activities. Take the ones who, in the 1140s, settled in Norway, which the Order's chroniclers thought of as the very ends of the earth. They came from fervent Yorkshire houses, Fountains and Kirkstead, and established communities near two trading centres, Bergen and Oslo. By a stroke of fortune, we have an idea of how the brothers saw their mission to this land converted to Christ just a hundred years before. They left an account of their labour. This speaks of the good zeal of Dom Ranulph, their first abbot, who was not just a shining example but furthermore, *gentem barbaram sub iugo Christi docuit mansuescere* – 'He taught a barbarous people to become gentle under the yoke of Christ.'[44]

The sentence moves me. These men set out from the north of England not just to be 'contemplatives'; they left to display the gentleness of Christ, the new life of the Gospel, to a people still marked by the violence of pagan ways. The Norwegian Cistercians went further in making themselves useful. The Order's international network, and the ability of individual monks, made them attractive to the nation's establishment. Time and again through the late twelfth, early thirteenth centuries, we find Cistercians acting as emissaries of kings and bishops. There is nothing to suggest that their observance was mitigated. But they did take on tasks one does not normally associate with cloistered monks. Why? It was what the time required.

I wonder if we are not too romantic in our appraisal of the Order's origins? Certainly, our Fathers were sincere and radical. They desired to live true monastic lives. They realized that desire. But they also engaged, surprisingly so, with the life of the Church and of society. We have considered a couple of examples. More could easily be found. Just think how the Order must have been affected by the part it played in the great propaganda machine that called forth the Second Crusade. Or think of the multiple relationships with non-monastic folk presupposed by the monks' enterprise 'in writing, chant, architecture and crafts, and in the skilful management of the land'.[45] The medieval monastery worked as a Roman *familia*, built upon concentric circles of graded attachment. An army of enterprising lay-brothers surrounded the core group of choir monks. Lay-helps assisted the lay-brothers. Artisans and farmers did work for the monks, bought their produce, or proposed their own for sale. Then, there were the guests and pilgrims. An abbey is not, cannot be, an isolated fortress. It is woven into a tight social fabric.

Analogous engagement was part of life even in the great eighteenth-century reinvention of Cistercian life, when Dom Augustin Lestrange and his companions laboured to fulfil the destiny of La Trappe in Swiss exile, establishing practices of hair-raising austerity. Even at La Valsainte, this reform-minded community established, of all things, a school. They assumed the care of children, and set up a kind of third order to assist with their work. This enterprise was a result, in part, of Lestrange's literalism. He wished to follow the Rule of St Benedict in all things. Benedict refers to the presence of children in the monastery. *Ergo* a house of strict observance should not be without them.[46]

There was, though, a slant to this perspective. Dom Augustin was a far-sighted man. He saw that his monks and nuns might have to pitch their tents in lands hostile to the contemplative calling. He considered it opportune for monks to perform some apostolic work, work that would be seen by all to be socially useful, of universal benefit. This, he thought, might assure fledgling communities a warmer welcome. The reformatory here at Mount Saint Bernard was part of this wider movement. So were the colleges of Roscrea and Mount Melleray in Ireland. The re-founding monks in Ireland and England were committed to the pure monastic life. But they were also committed to building up the local community. The monks of Mount Melleray, by their schools, increased literacy in Waterford in a beneficial impact that was strongly felt until quite recently. Cappoquin, I am told, still suffers from the closure of Mount Melleray's schools in the 1970s.

If we think of our African foundation, we see similar dynamics at work. From the start, the founders of Bamenda Abbey in Cameroon opened a dispensary. Medical care in mid-west Cameroon was scarce. Our brethren saw they could help. So they did. Long queues of the sick would form outside the main door, awaiting the monks' ministrations. This outreach developed into the herbal medicine department that, to this day, is Bamenda's chief breadwinner.

A parallel case is Tibhirine. The film *Of Gods and Men* has made Fr Luc, the good physician there, world famous. Monasteries help where they can to this day. Our sisters of Mvanda in Congo are hosts to a school of cooperative farming, trying to boost local agriculture. Some communities in poor regions manage their industries to provide employment for locals, who depend on monastic initiative. Scourmont in Belgium is a good example. Our Lady of the Lighthouse in Japan is another. The monks of Mepkin in the States minister to the needs of a spiritual desert by drawing people in through music festivals and exhibitions, extending the reach of hospitality. Our motherhouse of New Melleray sees its coffin factory as an apostolate, and rightly so, for that is how it is perceived, even by the unchurched. Accompanying people to the grave by the labour of their hands and by their prayers, the monks bear witness to Resurrection hope even more effectively than, say, by baking fruitcakes (though fruitcakes have their mission, too). It is right that we ask ourselves: what we are to do? What is God's call? What does the Church expect of us?

Apart from the tradition it springs from, each monastery has its particular grace, a grace of foundation. It springs from the specific vocation of the house, the vision that brought it into being. The founding of a monastery is no trivial matter. It corresponds to the needs of the soil in which it is planted, to the desire of the place for a monastic presence. Each story of foundation is different. Each leaves its mark (indelibly, I think) on the *genius loci*, on the gifts and limitations of a given monastery. 'Look to the rock from which you were hewn!' These words from Isaiah (51.1) refer not only to the very ancient past, to Cîteaux, Subiaco and Jerusalem. They refer no less to our local origins. So what is our foundation grace? What was the need, the love, the desire that called this particular house of prayer, our home, into being?

The reintroduction of Cistercian life to England owes more than we can say to the labours of our founder, Ambrose Phillipps de Lisle. He was on fire with a great matter: the conversion of England, no less. What de Lisle meant by this phrase, however, is not what it means in common currency. He did not envisage a Catholic crusade whereby one Christian communion would overtake another. His ideal was one of integration through healing and instruction. He thought the conversion of England would happen

> not by raising a new church, but by labouring to root out all heresy and hatred from the existing Churches of Canterbury and York, together with their kindred Dissenting bodies, and finally to restore all Christ-worshipping Englishmen to their former ancient Catholic condition of union with the Churches of the Continent and the Holy See of Rome.[47]

De Lisle was, in the modern, Catholic sense of that word, an ecumenist *ante litteram*. Note his stress on the need to uproot, not just heresy, but also hatred. Note his sense of a Catholic *condition*. He dreamt of England's return to a fullness of faith that had been compromised by strife and reformation, that believers might be reconciled in truth, that there might in truth be 'one fold, one shepherd'. De Lisle lived close to the heart of the Church. He found that heart wounded. He wished to see it healed and whole.

The founding of Mount Saint Bernard was linked to this vast, almost reckless concern. He wished the abbey to be an engine of catholicity, attractive to anyone drawn by a taste for what is genuine. His friend, Lord

Shrewsbury, did not at first see the use of what he called a 'regular monkery'. Surely a group of apostolic religious would better correspond to the needs of the times? De Lisle answered him in a strong letter: 'If you wish for an effective corps of Missionaries, I am certain that you cannot fix on a more serviceable class of Men than the Trappists, and I say this from experience.' They are devout, he explains, for 'the grand object of their Rule is the singing of the Divine office'. But this is not all:

> They devote themselves to missionary duties, and to the *corporal* as well as spiritual relief of the poor and sick, to whom they distribute medicines etc. – and this with a degree of ardour and assiduity which I never saw in secular Priests. Their abstemious life, their constant meditation, their profound study of spiritual books qualify them admirably as spiritual Directors, while it forms a fine commentary on the self-denying maxims of that Gospel which our Saviour came on earth to teach. Their houses are houses of spiritual retreat also for secular Gentlemen and Ecclesiasticks, and the good they do even in this way is very great.

De Lisle concludes on a pragmatic note. Wishing to reassure Shrewsbury, on whose benefaction he counted, he adds that the running costs of monks are low: 'you may support half-a-dozen Trappists on what would not satisfy one ordinary Priest'.

What emerges from this passage is confirmed elsewhere in the writings of de Lisle. It is a vision he must have discussed with our community's first superior, Fr Bernard Palmer and his small band of monks, settled in Charnwood, on Tynt Meadow, since 1835.

Our monastery of Our Lady and St Bernard was intended as a spiritual centre for the re-forming of Christian unity in England. It was to show forth the plenitude of Catholic life and faith. De Lisle was sure that such a testimony would be compellingly beautiful outwardly as well as inwardly; that it could not but attract true seekers of the truth. In this respect, it is interesting to note that de Lisle spontaneously harboured what is a key Cistercian insight. He saw that the physical environment we inhabit conditions our inward state of soul. He wished the very fabric of Mount Saint Bernard to offer all possible assistance in raising minds and hearts to God.

Everything about the monastery had to be noble, simple, attractive and well thought-out. De Lisle found a soul mate in Augustus Welby Pugin. The letters the two men exchanged about the building show an infinite attention to detail. Neither was inclined to reduce essence to appearance. Neither stood for superficial aestheticism. But both maintained that a criterion of truth must apply to visible forms as well as to invisible categories. The abbey was to be a sermon in stone, a proclamation of God's beauty and harmony. Like the monks' lives, it was to be authentic in every fibre.

De Lisle's biographer calls Mount Saint Bernard 'an appeal to the people of England'. It was to draw people in. De Lisle was delighted when it did. In 1842, looking forward, exhausted and broke, to the completion of his work, he wrote to Lord Shrewsbury: 'When the new Church is finished it will become the general *rendezvous* of all enquiring minds amongst the Anglicans.' The monastery, he was sure, had a role to play in God's providential plan for England. That is why he wished it to retain a degree of independence with regard to the Order as a whole, which, on the Continent, had to operate on different terms. De Lisle wished Mount Saint Bernard to be 'autocephalous and thoroughly *English*, adaptable to local requirements'. It was a disappointment to him when, in 1849, the community joined the international Cistercian Congregation of Strict Observance.

There is much to suggest that the monks, at least in part, assumed what de Lisle thought was their destiny. From the early days our house developed certain characteristics. The brethren had a concern for learning and the arts, and were surprisingly prolific. They had a great social conscience, manifest not just in their Reformatory, but in the aid they provided during the famine, when hundreds of people were fed every day at our guest-house door. Early visitors speak of a peculiar warmth of hospitality here, of a good-humoured, kindly spirit of welcome. And it is true to say, I think, that the community, while fully given to Cistercian authenticity, displayed some detachment with regard to the antics of strict observance, which they thought too French, too *trappiste*. There is a free-spirited cragginess about them that makes them fit well into this landscape of Charnwood rocks. We have a rich legacy to look back on. Grounded in it, we can confidently look forward.

FRAGILITY

Genesis concludes with Joseph's death. Exodus begins with the birth of Moses. In modern editions of the Bible, the two events occur on facing pages. We easily think of them as being close in time. It is useful, therefore, to meditate on the verses from Exodus we read at Vigils yesterday: 'The time that the people lived in Egypt was

430 years. After 430 years, on that very day, all the host of the Lord went out from Egypt' (12.40f.). The patriarchs displayed remarkable longevity. Even so, 430 years is a long time. Thinking 430 years back from today, we arrive at 1584. In that year, Parliament expelled the Society of Jesus; Walter Raleigh authorized the founding of a colony in Virginia; the theologian John Hales was born; the poet Jan Kochanowski died. The list could go on almost indefinitely, including events of greater or less significance, depending on our point of view. But most of us, I suspect, have to make some mental effort to think the year 1584 relevant to our present experience in 2014.

The Israelites who set out, staff in hand, laden with gifts of Egyptian gold, would have felt much the same with regard to Jacob's sons. We easily assume that time passed more quickly in earlier centuries. Of course, it didn't. It is doubtful whether prehistoric peoples found the abyss of the past less dark than we do. Still, we are prone to conflate situations that are, in fact, unconnected, like the lady I once met on a visit to a monastery in Brittany. She lectured me on St Thomas Aquinas's battle against Jansenism. The fact that almost four hundred years lay between the Angelic Doctor's death and the heyday of Jansenius did not impress her. She relegated both men to a nebulous 'past', void of divisions. Since they both lived long ago and were interested in the same sort of things, surely they met and quarrelled?

I am preparing to make what seems to me an important point. When, in the liturgical texts of this early part of Lent, we hear the Lord say, 'I have remembered my people', his remembrance was far from obvious to those generations of Israelites who wasted away in captivity and exile, thinking they had been forgotten. Some will have kept alive the flame of hope. Others will have snuffed it out, too tired, too fed up. For centuries, secret foundations were laid for future redemption in individual human hearts, by choices made in darkness. To trust or not to trust? To be faithful or to fall away? The faithful remnant, a motif central to Scripture, stands before us here for the first time. Thanks to it, there *was* a nation to remember and redeem 'in the fullness of time'. The ancestors' faith was honoured in their descendants. But that does not make the darkness they walked in less dense.

A monastery, an Order, has its own hallowed history, written with the finger of God. It shows striking analogies with the sacred narrative spread out before us in the Bible. In our history, too, there are signal moments of divine intervention, times at which God's power and presence are palpable.

The Cistercian family to which we belong has its own exodus to recall. When we think of the march on which our heroic brethren, monks and nuns, set out in 1798, walking from La Valsainte in Switzerland into Russia, we rightly feel a flush of filial pride. These were men and women of valour, whose legacy we consider our own. Who could doubt that a story with such extraordinary beginnings would continue in extraordinary ways?

The early members of our community took this pledge of prosperity for granted, bolstered by memories reaching back further still, to bursting cloisters at Rievaulx, Fountains and Garendon. Our fathers settled here to make the desert bloom, to restore the ruined temple. Theirs was the holy intransigence of Ezra and Nehemiah. Thanks to it, our monastery was solidly founded, and still stands. The tidal wave of vocations that washed into Mount Saint Bernard just before and after the Second World War seemed a further sign of divine favour and generous human response. Our community grew. It founded. It commanded a certain respect.

And now? From the select perspective I have just drawn up, the present can make us feel glum. Our choir stalls are bare. We can no longer do the kind of work we used to do. Recruitment is uncertain. The cemetery is filling up. Is there a future in store? Or is our only comfort now a prosperous past? We shall ask questions such as these only if we fall prey to the chronological delusion I described above; if we conjure up St Aelred's hundreds of monks, the heroes of La Valsainte, and post-war expansion in a single continuous sweep.

Why do we so easily forget the barren patches in between? When Rievaulx was dissolved, it housed 21 hapless monks. Garendon, in 1535, lay partly in ruins. The history of our own house has as many downs as ups. More than once there has been talk of closure. More than once we have been saved by generous help from outside, when on our own we could not have coped.

Every monk who has lived within these walls, we can safely assume, has desired to see the consolation of Israel. Not all of them have. Many will have lived their monastic lives in darkness, uncertain whether the great work to which they had unstintingly devoted their lives would survive. Thanks to these forgotten faithful monks who hoped against hope, who laboured without hope of reward, for the sheer joy of working in the vineyard, our monastery has made it till today. Will it survive? We do not know. Perhaps we should not care. By that I do not mean to invite indifference; rather to remind you, and myself, that the future is God's. We will enter it in so far as he gives it.

There is something intoxicating about the thought of standing on the threshold of a golden age, of new flourishing and expansion. Well, perhaps we are not, now, standing on such a threshold. Perhaps the years ahead will be years of struggle. Does it matter? Not much. What matters is only that we are faithful, that each day we renew, and act out of, the gift we have made of our lives. What matters is to keep the flame burning, to maintain the Cistercian grace alive, to serve the Lord Jesus with gladness, to invest our talents with audacity and faith-borne prudence. Then God will make of us what he will, and we shall praise him for it.

'Our Order', said St Aelred of Rievaulx, 'is the Cross of Christ.'[48] That is to say: our calling is to testify to Christ's redemptive gift. The purpose of our life is to make his power manifest. We know it thrives best in weakness. As we contemplate our fragility, therefore, let us not be afraid. It is on the humble that God looks; such he saves. Can a mother forget her sucking child? (cf. Isaiah 49.15). The better we know our weakness and need, the more truthfully we see ourselves; the less prone we are to that self-reliance which, in monasteries, can subtly turn into a form of corporate pride. Who knows whether our part is to thrive or simply to maintain a delicate continuity; to breathe on embers that will only burst into flame when we are gone, to warm and delight future generations we will not know? If the Lord gives fat years, let us praise him. If the years ahead are lean, let us praise him. Our task is to be faithful, truthful, trustful, joyful. What his task is, he knows best.

ISAAC OF STELLA

I have just reread Abbot Isaac of Stella's sermons for All Saints[49] with renewed astonishment. Isaac, born in England around the year 1100, is a thinker and preacher at once analytical and poetic. He speaks of what he knows from experience, so invites confidence as a sure guide. His six Sermons for All Saints are a compendious commentary on the Beatitudes, the foundation of all spiritual life. They provide food for thought in this season of Advent, as we strive to open our hearts, once again, to the coming of Jesus within us and among us.

'Seeing the crowds, Jesus went up onto the Mount' (Matthew 5.1). To hear him, Isaac says, we must do likewise. The crowd – 'turba' in Latin – is turbulent by nature. It jostles and distracts. It makes noise, sweeps us along willy-nilly, and causes us to end up, as likely as not, where we do not want to be. What is more, while we are *in* the crowd, part of it, we cannot see it. We take it for granted, assuming it is our natural habitat. To see ourselves for ourselves, we must step aside. That involves risk. Even though we may at times feel pressed, it is reassuring to be crowded. While we move with the crowd, we are absolved from the exacting exercise of freedom.

To be disciples of Jesus, we must first take leave of the turbulent mass about us. We must think for ourselves, take a stance. As we try to do just that, we make an uncomfortable discovery: we find we carry in our heart another, clamorous 'turba'. This interior crowd of thoughts and disordered desires, says Isaac, is more redoubtable than any outward crowd. So what can we do?

'Go forth, brother', Isaac tells us, 'and follow Jesus. He came down to you [from heaven] that you might ascend *above* yourself, to reach him *in* yourself!' This seems nonsensical until he explains: 'Brother, you must set up a hiding place within to which you can flee from yourself, if you wish to pray to your Father in secret.' God became man to seek us as we are, in our nature. Our humanity is the pledge of our redemption. By virtue of baptism, we have a claim on our Redeemer. All he asks in order to prepare a dwelling for himself in us is that we make that claim.

We can think of ourselves in terms of two distinct interior arenas. One arena is our natural self. It is noisy, chaotic, curious, drawn in different directions. The other arena is our supernatural self, the wellspring of peace and holy leisure. It is oriented, still, drawn as a magnet to Christ, the Prince of Peace. It is in this second arena, opening up to eternity, that beatitude is found; the trouble is, we look for bliss elsewhere, outside. We like to scurry around in the undergrowth of passion, and do not even see the ascending heavenward path flanked by angels robed in light.

To ascend with Christ, says Isaac, we need to travel light. Think of Elisha. He slaughtered five yokes of oxen to follow God's call freely (1 Kings 19.21). He set us an example. We may object: 'When I entered the monastery, I left all!' True, but we easily start re-collecting. Simeon the New Theologian remarks: 'If you throw dust over the flames of a blazing furnace, you put it out. In the same way, all the cares of life and all your shabby attachments, even the most trivial, annihilate the fervour that was alight in your heart at the beginning.'[50] We do not want that to happen. But we know how easily, surreptitiously, it can.

'On the outside', Isaac goes on, 'you are an animal, made in the image of this world. Within, you are a man in the image of God. That is how you can be deified!' The terms of this dichotomy are so flabbergasting we may be tempted to treat them as figures of speech. Theology teaches us otherwise. We have the choice either to live as beasts do, or, by God's grace, to become like God. Such is the stature of humanity redeemed.

Isaac knows what effort is called for in order to seek God single-heartedly. He says as much in a telling phrase: *Eia, fratres, seria res agitur, virile est quod aggressi sumus*. We could render this in English as follows. 'Watch out, brothers, this is a serious business. What we've undertaken is a manly task.' Does the bit about manliness make you cringe? It is a notion we are uncomfortable with, these days. Discomfort arises for two reasons.

The first pertains to the imperative of inclusiveness. We are conditioned to think that gender-specific, specifically male-gendered, language is chauvinistic. It is meritorious and right to be cautious in the use of language, but one can go too far. I doubt whether Isaac's adjective 'virile' would get past an editor's scrutiny today. As likely as not it would be rendered as 'courageous', 'daring', or something like that – and would that be such a loss? Yes it would. But let us first consider the second reason why our society is unhappy with 'manliness'.

It is commonly said that the Western world is in the throes of a crisis of masculinity. I think it is true. Western man is unsure of his place in the world. What is more, he feels he is expected to apologize for past oppression. Again, there is here, at heart, something good. Our modern sense of the equality of the sexes, of the fact that one is not superior to the other, is a step forward for humanity. What is more, it enables men to discover new dimensions of their role as men. Coming from what is probably the world's most egalitarian country, I feel I can speak with some authority. Sweden and Norway are the only places I know where gentlemen's loos in airports are fitted with fold-down nappy-changing tables. Norwegian fathers get statutory time off work when their children are born. That is simply terrific.

And yet, as men discover that much that women have traditionally done, they can do too, they are left perplexed. What is their particular role? Men have ended up in something of a mess. For one thing, the blurring of gender boundaries gives rise to projections of manliness that are barbaric and embarrassing. As if to compensate for loss of status, men have invented an icon of themselves that is charged with aggressivity. To be a 'real man' in our world is to be set on sexual conquest, to live by appetites, to be reckless and rich, and to depend on no one; that is, to be ruthless.

Isaac addresses the fix we are in. He and his contemporaries, looking back to antiquity, had well-thought-out ideas of manly comportment. The way they understood it may sound unfamiliar. For ancient and medieval people, masculinity and femininity were understood as poles of a single spectrum, opposites existing in tension within each of us. These poles must be balanced if we are to live grown-up, free, fruitful lives as mature women and men.

An image of Plato's helps us enter the mind-set of our Fathers. He was their favourite philosopher. In the *Phaedrus*, Plato likened the soul to a chariot drawn by two horses. One stands for the moral impulse of our passionate nature (such as anger, which *can* be turned into righteous indignation); the other stands for irrational passions (such as carnal lusts and appetites). Both horses champ at the bit, pulling in opposite directions. They get nowhere except by direction of their winged charioteer, representing reason, our capacity for thoughtful discernment. If the horses obey him, the chariot rises towards the heavens, approaching divine contemplation. If instead they disobey, it crashes onto earth, unable to rise above the level of clods.[51]

This summary does not do Plato justice, evidently. But it will do for now. It leaves us with three elements to consider: the potentially rational passions, the irrational passions, and reason. Indeed, the Fathers commonly divide the soul into three parts. In Latin these are referred to, most of the time, as *animus*, *anima*, and *mens* or *ratio*. This model was susceptible to further reduction in a move inspired by Greek grammar. The Greek for 'soul', *psyche*, is a feminine noun. The Greek for 'reason', *logos*, by contrast, is masculine. The passions as a whole, on this model, stand as female, while the principle of intellect is male. All of us, whether we are men or women, need to find a stable, fruitful equilibrium between these two poles.

With all this in mind, let us return to Isaac of Stella. We are in for a surprise. For on this reading, our modern-day icon of maleness, the lager-swilling, erotically insatiable, anger-exuding lad, would be called effeminate. He is a slave to animal passions. The manly man, by contrast, is one whose appetites are governed by grace-inspired reason. He is gentle, responsible and peaceful. He is chaste and pure. He submits self-will to ideals and invests himself for others.

Isaac's position is arduous, but wonderfully freeing and inspiring. Just listen to the following passage, from the fifth sermon for All Saints. It sets out what is needed for union with God by drawing a parallel with physical love:

> In the case of one who clings to flesh by un-manned, weak voluptuousness, the spirit itself becomes almost wholly flesh; the two who cling carnally one to the other *are* but one flesh. Is it not fitting, then, that one who with masculine heart and virile mind pours himself out in God, by a love no less, oh no!, but chaster and purer, to the point of holding back not a bit, keeping nothing, stripped of self; that such a man should be one spirit with the One to whom he clings?

The man who lives by desire is portrayed as 'un-manned'. The one who, out of longing for God, empties himself is called masculine and virile.

We see, now, the sense of the passage we set out from, where Isaac reminds us that, as monks, we have embraced a 'manly task'. We have promised to give all, to renounce self-satisfaction. We have promised to pursue the inner life with verve, preferring nothing to Christ, who is our Logos. So we must, on these terms, show ourselves men. That is how we shall become fit instruments for God on this earth. That is how, in our hearts, we shall conceive the Son of God.

This is a pleasing paradox, only conceivable in Christian thought, with its constantly surprising synthesis of opposites: by being manly, we shall correspond to the Marian dimension of our call, saying Yes to the coming of the Lord into our lives, placing all that is ours at his disposal. 'A man is born to work,' says Isaac of Stella. We have placed our hand on the plough. We have resolved to build God's kingdom here, in this humble monastery. God grant us courage, strength and manliness to stay faithful to the end.

How do we progress along these lines? Isaac's response shows how rooted he is in monastic self-understanding. For many of the early Fathers, the purpose of monasticism was the pursuit of purity of heart. Isaac says much the same. He points to the sixth beatitude: 'Blessed are the pure in heart. They shall see God.' As contemplatives, we long for vision. In the words of the Psalms, we give voice to that longing constantly: 'Let us see, O Lord, your mercy' (84.7); 'Lord, show us your face' (80.19); 'When shall I enter and see?' (41.2). As long as we keep that yearning alive, we shan't veer too far from the straight, narrow path.

Fundamentally, Isaac's notion of spiritual life is simple. He would have approved of a remark once made by Dame Laurentia McLachlan of Stanbrook. Finding a nun distraught after meeting a prying, too zealous director of conscience, a priest demanding to know on which floor of the Interior Castle she abode, Abbess Laurentia was dismissive. 'Can't you tell him you want *plain God*?' she asked. Often she cited the Psalter: *Proponebam Dominum in conspectu meo semper*; 'I shall keep the Lord ever in my sight'

(Psalm 15.8). That, she said, is the one indispensable star we need to steer by.[52] It will lead us to our heart's desire. As an orientation it is sane. But daunting. Do I keep the Lord before my eyes at all times? Or do I prefer, now and again, to look away, to seek distraction, amusement or licence for self-indulgence?

Isaac knows that the purity of heart required for such vision must be conquered and won. Our hearts are damaged by sin. They have been partially disfigured. It is the nature of sin to make us miss the mark. Our hearts are no longer set by default on God as the object of their longing. Our inner compass needle hovers. The primary task in hand is to restore our hearts to good working order, that they may be fit to see, hear and obey, and so to love.

That is how they will expand. That is how we shall proceed, fleet-footed and with joy, on the path of Christ's commandments, made whole by the power of Christ's love. To purify our heart, says Isaac, is a twofold task. We must guide it towards virtue. We must guide it towards truth. Virtue and truth. We must consider these objectives in turn.

Isaac's teaching on virtue is thoroughly traditional. He orchestrates the drama of conversion, however, in a manner quite his own. He likens humankind, you and me, to the man going down from Jerusalem to Jericho. 'This man set on descent', he says, 'is the common Adam.' He is Everyman. Isaac refuses to see him as a victim: 'It was of his own will, foolishly, that he started his descent. When he fell among robbers, he got only his due. For Adam could have remained in the peace for which he was created, a peace rich in all manners of good, safe from danger.' The Fathers were fond of etymologies. Isaac asks us to remember, with him, the meaning of 'Jerusalem': 'Vision of Peace'.

Why did Adam not stay there? Because of the wanton attractions of the plain. We know what the lowlands stand for in Scripture: tepidity and compromise. The root cause of unhappiness is our unwillingness to stay fixed on God. We prefer other things to him. We like to see our small desires satisfied, and end up languishing, estranged from our Creator. Each time we choose lesser goods, we're distracted from him who is Goodness itself. Thus Isaac, like the monks of old, sees pride as the wellspring of sin-sickness.

Pride equals self-love. It makes me prefer my own desire to the will and commandment of God. Pride gives birth to envy, though this term inadequately renders Isaac's *invidia*. He defines it as 'hatred of the happiness of others' – a terrifying state of soul. If I surrender to it, not only am I obsessed with satisfying my own idea of contentment; I want only myself to be happy, and resent it when others get their share. Thus anger follows, a dark 'disturbance of the soul' that makes me restless, touchy, resentful, hyper-sensitive to what I see as slights. Sadness sets in. Then I start amassing little consolations and become avaricious. Before I know it, I slide into gluttony and lust. This, says Isaac, is what happens once we turn our eyes away from the Lord, abandoning the peace of Jerusalem.

How can we find our way back? As monks we have many road signs to steer by. If, when the bell goes for Office, we think, 'I've something else to do' or 'I don't feel like going'; if we neglect community exercises; if we skimp on private prayer and *lectio*; if we prefer private projects to shared enterprise; if we hoard food and drink; if we nurse old resentments and feel sorry for ourselves: then we are bound, not for Jerusalem, but for the fetid plains of Jericho. We turn away from the crystalline altitudes of God and retreat into the moist armpit of self.

What wonder if we end up feeling listless, irritated and disappointed? We shall have handed ourselves over to robbers! We must be watchful, then, says Isaac, and keep climbing. The ascent to Jerusalem is an ascent towards our higher potential, the pinnacle of soul where God awaits us. As we rise, we are sustained by virtue. Virtue is not lavender-scented and dull. It is manly, fresh and exciting. Its root meaning is 'strength'. Why choose to droop?

The search for virtue must be matched by a single-minded search for truth. Intended is truth about self, no doubt. It is the only foundation for spiritual life. But as the scholar he was, Isaac goes further. He points to the constraints we may be subject to by having wrong ideas of ultimate realities. We follow the effects of such deception in our refectory reading of Avery Dulles's memoirs.[53] Dulles recounts how his early philosophical assumptions blocked him from faith. He speaks of his materialism: the assumption that some kind of *stuff* is the origin of everything, that 'spiritual' values are constructs of the mind. He speaks of his relativism: the assumption that one creed, one ethical code is as good as another, fashioned by human beings out of self-interest. These assumptions are shared today by almost all our contemporaries in the West. It would be a miracle if they hadn't crept into our thinking, too, just a bit. So we may find ourselves, like Dulles, hampered in spiritual progress by lazily assimilated, unthought-through falsehoods.

We may carry more than we like to admit of the baggage of nihilism. Do we have space in our minds for absolute Truth?

Isaac of Stella, like Dulles, bids us spare no effort in tidying up our thoughts, in seeking insight. We have magnificent resources at disposal: the Scriptures, the Magisterium, the Church's patrimony of rigorous thinking interiorized in prayer. What is asked of us is this: a will to keep learning coupled with sufficient humility of mind to recall just how little we know and understand, how far God exceeds our expectations. If we proceed along these lines, growing in virtue and letting God's light shine on exercised minds, we can hope to rise up towards the new Jerusalem. There we shall see the fullness of Truth in the radiance of Christ's face. There we shall know it in love outpoured. The closer we draw to that vision, that Vision of Peace, the more connatural will be the attitude required for true happiness and freedom, the attitude that speaks, connaturally, 'Let it be to me according to your word' (Luke 1.38).

THE LAST DAYS OF ROME

'No one should presume to relate to anyone else what he saw or heard outside the monastery, because that causes the greatest harm.' Such is St Benedict's injunction to 'brothers sent on a journey'.[54] I intend to disobey. This week I travelled to Downside to give talks to the community there. On the journey, I saw, in the secular press, things that made me think, things I think we ought all to think about. I would like to share them with you.

A fact of current public life that may have escaped our notice is a national campaign to unearth and investigate historic allegations of child sex-abuse. The Home Secretary made the matter a priority after the press reported the disappearance of a dossier compiled 30 years ago about paedophiles in parliament: an inquiry was called for in the 1980s, but was covered up, it seems, and forgotten. The report has unleashed something near hysteria. The front page of *The Times* on Thursday, 17 July 2014, revealed that 'tens of thousands' of allegations are under review, touching men involved in politics, health care, education, the Church of England, and many other sectors of public life. What are we to make of this?

The first thing to say is that it is good, indeed essential, that anyone who has hurt and corrupted the trust of an underage person, boy or girl, is held answerable. We are touching a sickness that runs deep in our society; more deeply, I dare say, than anyone had thought. It needs to become manifest, however awful the process is. Paedophile misconduct, long associated almost exclusively with Catholic clergy, is seen to be a far-reaching problem. But let's avoid any trace of smugness. What we are dealing with is a tragic, miserable reality. And abuse is especially reprehensible on the part of a consecrated person, ordained to be Christ's ambassador. The humiliation of the present time is a fact of life for the Church. We should not try to shake it off. We must learn from it and heed it as a summons to conversion.

A second point, turning from effects to causes: what sort of malaise is it that corrodes and corrupts the relationship of adults to children? What is it that turns relationships of trust and responsibility into relationships of predatory desire? What distortions creep into human minds to suggest that power can be used to satisfy lust? For power is a key factor in unequal relationships, such as that between adults and children, especially when the adult has a claim to status and influence. The question, I know, is so unpleasant that we do not really want to look at it. Given the epidemic scale of incidents, however, we cannot afford not to. There is a sickness abroad in our society. We must diagnose it in order, next, to strive to heal it.

A third point concerns the broader impact on society. Douglas Murray hits the nail on the head in a column in this week's *Spectator*. Rehearsing the long list of scandals that, in recent years, has beset the BBC, the NHS, the Churches, any number of MPs, and so forth, he remarks: 'Rarely since the last days of Rome can there have been such a dearth of authority in a society. One by one, in the lifespan of most people in Britain, the institutions which once defended and epitomised our country have fallen and now appear unable to get up again.'[55]

Murray is concerned about the vacuum that ensues. It leaves us, he maintains (and I think he is right) vulnerable to the power of dubious charisma:

> The more one considers modern Britain, the clearer it becomes that public virtue has become a ghost town. Almost anyone might now move in and declare themselves sheriff. We are over-ready for some figure of apparent purity, meaning, and drive to wipe it all away.

The last century gives ghastly examples to prove that this is no vain warning.

What to me is particularly striking is the line drawn to a specific epoch in the past: 'Rarely since the last days of Rome ...' It is something I think of a great deal: the parallels between our times and the fourth and fifth centuries are often eerie. If you admit the comparison, the current societal crisis is brought close to home for us as monks. For those two centuries of decline were also the centuries during which our form of life was founded and decisively developed.

One reason why monasticism flourished in the dying empire was precisely this: that the monks, who abandoned all to live lives of great austerity, emerged as credible authorities in an age that had lost its bearings. By their sacrifices, charity and prayer, they stood for a different kind of world, a different way of being human that, by force of example, attracted hosts of followers. We are sometimes drawn to smile at what we think of as excesses in early monasticism: at the stylites on their pillars, at dendrites living in trees, at anchorites befriending bears and lions.

Think twice before dismissing them as laughable. If monks went to such lengths it was partly, no doubt, because the world in which they lived had come so utterly to distrust all claims to truth. In order to show that what they held to be truth *was* true, they had to prove it with their lives in ways that made a difference. What was it about the best of monks and nuns that impressed late Romans in Egypt, Mesopotamia, Byzantium and Gaul? It was their verifiable integrity, their consistently lived witness to the profession they made with their lips. In an age of lost illusions, such testimonies struck like rods of lightning.

This concerns our mission as monks today. I am not suggesting we build treehouses. Nor am I suggesting we promote ourselves as paragons of virtue. No! I point to the responsibility we have to live upright, truthful, whole, holy lives. Our contemporaries have been serially let down by people they thought they could trust. They are cynical, therefore, and often rather cruel. This doesn't mean they no longer long for someone to rely on. Our task is to show that such a One exists.

By our dedication we are called to manifest that Christ is real, that he heals and saves, that his love is the substance of our lives, no fairy tale. Our world is in crisis. Anarchic secularists are pitted against ideological theocrats, often on the same turf, both unimaginably armed, both influenced, whether or not they admit it, by the West's broad-gated gospel of selfish materialism. Untold masses of women, men and children are living through utter anguish, in warfare, disease and want. How do we live through times of such disappointment, decadence and fear?

One option is to turn our mind to something else. It was what the lady did who sat next to me on the bus to Stratton-on-the-Fosse. Having raced through the international news in the *Daily Mail*, she stayed engrossed in a full-page article about Eric, a black Labrador who got his head stuck between two boulders while out for a walk on a beach in Cornwall. I am sympathetic to Eric, of course, but the escapism that kind of story provides is no option for monks. St Benedict calls on us to be soldiers. We have an urgent battle to fight. A battle for goodness and truth; a battle against violence, bigotry and hatred; a battle against perversions of will and desire. So let us put on, with resolve, the armour of faith, remembering that prayer is a powerful weapon in these menaced, menacing times.

3

THE HEART'S EXPANSION

A PILLAR IN GOD'S TEMPLE

I have been asked to explain the phrase I have chosen as my abbatial motto: *Columna in templo Dei* (Revelation 3.12). I owe it to a discovery I made shortly after I had entered the community. An obituary had appeared on the notice board from one of our abbeys in America. I have often regretted that I did not make a copy of it, for I cannot remember it exactly. But it has become, as I recall it, a crucial reference.

I remember neither the monk's name nor which house he was from. I remember he had served for long years as prior and had been a paragon of goodness – dependable, reliable, always *there*. This legacy, the obituarist noted, was in keeping with the orientation of his dead brother's charism, for he had taken as his monastic motto precisely this phrase from the Apocalypse: 'a pillar in God's temple'.

The choice puzzled me. I re-read the obituary over several days to work out what it might have meant to the monk who chose it. A pillar seemed an unattractive model. I thought of being cast 'from pillar to post'. I thought what a lifeless thing a pillar is. It doesn't breathe. It doesn't move. It doesn't do anything. Pillars are often in the way. More than once I have found myself walking around some church or stately building, looking at paintings or an ornate ceiling, to find my musings brought to a halt as I walked into a pillar in my path, trying for sheer embarrassment to contain the expletives tripping to my tongue.

Why would a monk find this stagnant, potentially hostile object a sign to emulate? The Spirit is dynamic! With time, I think I have come to understand. Not only that; I find the image of the pillar ever more attractive. I often return to the passage from the third chapter of the Apocalypse in which the phrase occurs.

It so happened that we had that passage read at Vigils on 16 April, the day of our abbatial election. When later, in Chapter, the election result was announced and I was asked, 'Do you accept?' I thought of that steadfast old monk and his pillar. It seemed his motto had been passed on to me as a guiding star for my ministry. So I decided to assume it. As a sign of direction to myself, I will endeavour to place my life during this time within the logic of the saying, 'a pillar in God's temple'.

St John's pillar is mentioned in the sixth of his Letters to the Seven Churches, the one addressed to Philadelphia, a town upcountry from Ephesus. Its very name conferred hopes of a noble destiny. The Greek noun *philadelphia* means 'love of the brethren', the essence of a Christian assembly. In Norway, Pentecostal halls of worship are commonly called 'Philadelphia'. In that Christian idiom, 'love of the brethren' is synonymous with 'church'.

The biblical Philadelphians are praised by John for their commitment to the truth and their allegiance to his 'word of patient endurance' (Revelation 3.10). We pick up a

Benedictine accent at this point. Lived truth is a function of sticking it out. The context for the exhortation is the prospect of the Lord's return. Continue to keep faith, says the Lord through the apostle; and be prepared for trials. Then he goes on: 'He who conquers, I will make him a pillar in the temple of my God; never shall he go out of it, and I will write on him the name of my God, and the name of the city of my God [...], and my own new name. He who has an ear, let him hear' (3.12f.). Very well, let us try.

What is the principal function of a pillar? It is to hold the roof up. A lot of pillars from antiquity are now free-standing. Think of the Parthenon. But they were not designed as such. They have ended up solitary because the roof is no more. But it used to be there. A pillar creates a space where life can flourish protected from the elements, where people can feel safe and comfortable. An abbot must fulfil an analogous function. His ministry is geared towards others' well-being.

His pastoral staff reminds him of that. He is to ward off wolves and send hirelings packing. He is to draw in the stray, to shut out winds of dissension and falsehood. If he does, he will generate about him, like a solid pillar, a wide-open space; a space where it is good to be, where one breathes freely; a hospitable space. He will, like a pillar, point upwards, raising minds and hearts to higher things.

Of course, a pillar will only be effective if it has a firm foundation. A pillar on a bed of sand is of no use. A pillar must be built on rock. That rock, for us, is Christ. St Benedict is emphatic: 'the abbot must never teach or decree or command anything that would deviate from the Lord's instruction'. Whatever the abbot commands, he must practise.[56] He should always strive to live by and communicate God's Word, living and breathing the Scriptures.[57]

I learnt recently that this is what the mitre signifies. Its two lappets stand for the Old and New Testaments, its domed shape for God's all-containing Word. Far from elevating its bearer, as if it were an Oriental crown, it reminds him that he is a man submitted to authority, obliged at all times to practise St Benedict's *ausculta*, 'Listen, my son!',[58] then to obey.

Built on rock, pointing upwards, holding the roof, a pillar must sustain much tension. I am struck by the number of times St Benedict says the abbot should 'bear'. He is to bear with the weak; the lost he is to bear back to the fold; he bears responsibility for the brethren's progress; if the monks, through his neglect, make no progress, he will bear the blame; at the last he will have to bear God's judgement.[59] He must, therefore, be steadfast and faithful.

That is the meaning of the ring put on his finger. 'Will you be faithful?' asks the bishop in the solemn rite of blessing. He then goes on: 'Take this ring, the seal of fidelity.'[60] The circular shape is, of all nature's geometry, the most resistant. It lets tension flow so that it does not get arrested and cause breakage. Pillars tend to be round. For all their rock-like solidity, they suggest a flowing movement. The abbot is asked to surrender to this flow, aware that his pledge is pledged on the fidelity of him who is God's Yes (2 Corinthians 1.20), 'who opens and no one can shut' (Revelation 3.7).

The pillar of the *Apocalypse* is inscribed with three names: the name of God and of the new Jerusalem, also the 'new name' of him who walks among the seven golden lampstands. One is fit to be incorporated into God's temple in so far as one is wholly claimed by God. How often St Benedict reminds the abbot that his office is not an entitlement but a vicarious commission. The abbot is to be Christ's agent. To carry and support as he ought, he, too, must be inscribed with Christ's name.

That, surely, is why he is given a cross to wear, as a constant reminder of him whose place, unworthily, he holds, whom he must obey, whose words he is to speak, whose mercy he is to transmit. The cross is a reminder of who really carries. How true it is, but how often we must relearn it: we cannot bear anything unless we're carried in the first place! To be a pillar in God's temple is to have the sign of the cross before one's eyes, upon one's heart, at all times.

When the Rule asks us to prefer nothing to Christ's love, it is really being quite pragmatic. Prefer nothing else, for nothing else can carry. Christ's love bears all things, believes all things, hopes all things, endures all things (cf. 1 Corinthians 13.7). It makes the weak strong, the fearful brave. The abbot in particular is to manifest that truth by his life. But so are we all. No structure of importance is upheld by *one* pillar alone. We are all called to bear, to help each other, each bearing his own load yet carrying each other's burdens, never wavering from the place assigned to us by Christ our Lord in this mysterious communion we call Mount Saint Bernard. He called us here by name. He has set his seal upon us. Asked, he will give us grace to be worthy, dependable pillars in a temple destined to be filled with his glory.

MURMURING

No vice is condemned more strictly by St Benedict than that of murmuring. Early on in the Rule, he establishes, by way of general principle, that the monk must 'not be a murmurer'.[61] In the following chapter, on obedience, the theme is developed at length. This is natural. It is when obedience makes real demands that self-will asserts itself, and may erupt in a murmurous belch. St Benedict won't have it. Murmuring incurs an immediate warning. If it goes uncorrected, says he, it must be punished. It is one of the misdemeanours that qualifies for excommunication. We know all this and take it to heart. Why is it, then, that murmuring stays a persistent temptation?

When I looked up 'murmur' in the Lewis & Short *Latin Dictionary* to check its etymology, I discovered it is an exceedingly ancient word, derived from Sanskrit *marmara* through Greek *murmurō*. Murmuring, in other words, has been around since the beginning of recorded evidence. The root sense describes a quality of sound, even as we use it still to describe, say, the murmur of traffic. The sound in question is usually neither pleasant nor reassuring. A murmur is full of foreboding.

Latin writers used cognates of 'murmur' to describe the distant roaring of a lion, the onset of a wind presaging a storm, or the rumble of an earthquake. There is a hidden violence in murmuring. This semantic charge enables it, by seamless progression, to assume a tropological sense as the utterance of passive aggression.

When someone murmurs, he or she assumes, at least implicitly, a posture of rebellion. Of course, a murmur is vague and indistinct. One can hear *that* someone murmurs but rarely *what* is murmured. Murmuring is different from speaking up, which is an honest business. What makes murmuring noxious is its quality of stealth, its procedure of secret undermining.

This is how we encounter the word in Scripture. In the Latin Bible familiar to St Benedict, the first mention of murmuring occurs in Exodus 15.24, where, after several aborted attempts to leave Egypt, thwarted by Pharaoh, the Israelites have at last embraced the path to freedom. They have crossed the Red Sea, seeing Egypt's chariots drowned in their wake, 'sinking like a stone'. Moses' exultant canticle, which the Church sings at each Easter Vigil, takes up two-thirds of this fifteenth chapter. It celebrates the Lord's mighty deeds. Its thrust is this: it is *the Lord* who has set Israel free. *He* has 'triumphed gloriously'. *He* has thrown 'the horse and its rider' into the sea. *His* right hand 'shatters the enemy'. *He* – and this is the crunch – has given proof of his 'steadfast love', leading forth the people *he* has redeemed. The song (15.1-18) ends on a note of jubilant hope: 'You will bring [your people] in and plant them on your holy mountain, the place, O Lord, which you have made for your dwelling.'

The people who earlier (4.31) prostrated themselves in adoration at the mere mention of God's promise of redemption now know that his promise carries, that the Lord does move among them, a pillar of cloud and of fire, powerful to save. The exodus has vindicated Israel's hope. It has verified that the Lord acts on their behalf.

Yet the people, still with Red Sea mud on their feet, soon changed their tune. Having walked for three days, they came to Marah, where the water was undrinkable, too bitter. At this, the people murmured against Moses. They said, 'What are we to drink?' (15.24). Striking here is the change of perspective. As long as they were still looking back, recalling their adventure so far, including the crossing of the Red Sea, the people acknowledged God as their guide. When faced with present suffering, however, when the journey through the desert, begun joyfully, makes them thirsty, they abandon their supernatural outlook. They look around for someone to blame. Moses is the obvious target. They vent their grievance on him, murmuring, then asking, 'How will you fix this?' God is praised for good things that happen; difficult things are ascribed to human incompetence. The name of the place, Marah, means 'bitterness'. Bitter is Israel's complaint. Marah water will for all time symbolize murmuring, which leaves a foul taste in the mouth, cannot quench thirst and suffocates hope.

Moses cries out to the Lord. The Lord in response shows him a tree, telling him to cast it into the water – not just a twig or a bit of bark, but the whole tree. At once the water is sweetened. Israel can drink. The memory of this event will later inspire the Church's contemplatives, who recognized the tree as foreshadowing Christ's cross by which sin is forgiven. The rebellion of Marah, the proto-murmur, is thereby linked to our sinful condition as such, our fallen humanity, and rightly so. For what is sin, if not a lack of faith and trust, the presumption of assuming that God cannot, will not, reach or help us? God's oracle to Moses at Marah, once the people had drunk, merits attention.

> If you will diligently hearken to the voice of the Lord your God, and do what is right in his eyes, and give heed to his commandments and keep all his statutes, I will put none of the diseases upon you which I put upon the Egyptians; for I am the Lord, your healer (15.26).

The first plague that struck Egypt was the poisoning of water. So at Marah, the people assumed: God is doing to us what he did to our enemies. 'How could you think such a thing?' retorts the living God. He reminds them that their journey is a journey of faith, whose map is a covenant. From the outset of the Lord's revelation to Moses, he had stated his intention 'to bring them up out of [Egypt] to a good and broad land, a land flowing with milk and honey' (3.8). Is he not a trustworthy God? Is he not the God of their fathers, Abraham, Isaac and Jacob? He has proved that he fulfils his promises. The point of hardening Pharaoh's heart was to show that God's power can vanquish human opposition. The point of making the Red Sea waters stand 'like a wall' (14.29) was to show that the forces of nature are subject to a providential plan. God is a faithful God. But will Israel have faith?

At this crucial juncture the people are reminded that God's saving work is premised on their loyalty. They have entered a covenant. A covenant, by definition, is two-sided. God treats Israel like a man fit to give his word, expected to keep it. Israel's murmuring gives God an occasion to rehearse the 'If' on which the covenant is premised. God will keep them, save them, heal them *if* they listen to his word, do what is right, keep his commandments. This includes going forward in faith even when their path passes through waterless places. They must walk, and not murmur.

There is a twist in this tale, of course. It occurs in the very last verse of Exodus 15, in an observation mentioned as if by the way. In fact it gives the key to the whole narrative. Having moved on from Marah, we are told, 'the people came to Elim where there were twelve springs of water and seventy palm trees; and they encamped there'. Israel's murmuring had erupted on the threshold of a delightful oasis towards which God was leading them. They had bitterly complained, 'we have no water', just as God was about to surprise them with bountiful springs and shade in sweet abundance. In this there is a perennial lesson.

Having refreshed themselves in Elim, a garden land in the middle of the desert, Israel set out again 'on the fifteenth day of the second month after their departure from Egypt' (16.1). Only six weeks had passed since they saw the Red Sea part to let them through, then fold back to submerge their pursuers. The Hebrew text of Exodus 14, where that story is told, brings out an important motif that easily gets lost in translation. Taking stock, as it were, after the crossing, the author sums up the saving events as follows: 'On that day, the Lord saved [the verbal root is *yod-shin-'ayin*, which gives rise to the name *Y'shua*, that is, 'Jesus'] Israel from the hand of Egypt [...], and Israel saw the Lord's great hand by which he wrought among the Egyptians' (14.30f.). The Lord's great hand 'wrought'. But how?

By means of another's hand. To part the Red Sea waters, the Lord said to Moses, 'stretch out your hand over the sea and divide it' (14.16). To cause the walls of water to collapse on Egypt's chariots, he told Moses again, 'Stretch out your hand that the water may come back' (14.26). In other words: to save Israel from the *hand* of Egypt, the Lord's *great hand* worked marvels through the *hand* of Moses. No wonder that, as a result, the people 'feared the Lord, and believed in the Lord and in his servant Moses' (14.31). This profession of faith was subject to a blip three days later, at Massah, as we have seen. But surely, with that, the people had learnt their lesson? Not at all. Their murmuring reached fever pitch in the very next stage of the journey.

Once out of Elim, the people entered the wilderness of Sin, 'which is between Elim and Sinai' (16.1). We know what graces awaited them at Sinai. The people could not have known; neither, it turns out, did they care. For the 'whole congregation', all of them, 'murmured against Moses and Aaron' there, in the wilderness. They said: 'Would that we had died by the hand of the Lord in the land of Egypt when we sat by the fleshpots and ate bread to the full; for you have brought us out into this wilderness to kill this whole assembly with hunger' (16.3). With these claims, murmuring enters a new dimension. It reveals its true face more fully. We have seen how the murmurer seeks to apportion blame to others. This tends to go hand in hand, as in this passage, with a claim to victimhood for himself.

'You're destroying us', is Israel's message to Moses. 'We were fine where we were until you interfered and snared us into this crazy scheme destined to destroy us!' Forgotten now long days spent under a pitiless sun, gathering stubble for straw. Forgotten Pharaoh's foremen with their whips. Forgotten the killing of Israel's male progeny. What was felt to be 'cruel bondage' then (6.9) comes to seem, in retrospect, a not uncomfortable existence. In the context of the wilderness of Sin, no one recalls that Israel's united voice once 'cried out for help to the Lord' (2.23), who 'saw their affliction' (3.7), promising to save them, to bring them up, away. The only cry that matters now is that of empty stomachs, demanding to be filled.

In human terms, the dynamic at work is one we observe in impatient children. You may have travelled with children who, at some point, get too tired, too hungry or too bored, so start wailing, wanting whatever it is they want *now*. It is little use trying to make Johnnie see that the Boeing 747 is cruising above the Sahara and there is no way of getting his blue teddy. He just cries more loudly: 'Now!' If you are mum or dad you must think up a ruse of diversion. If you are the passenger in front of Johnnie, as I was on my last trip to Cameroon, you must sit tight and wait, pushing your ear plugs further in, and breathe deeply.

Such behaviour in children is annoying but understandable. In adults it is pathetic. Yet do we not, almost all, yield to it from time to time? If we look at Israel between Elim and Sinai, frustration has cancelled out all sense of perspective. The people are so absorbed in present need that there is no space on their horizon for the future or the past, for where they've come from, where they're going. Anything outside the present moment seems a blur, a vaguely attractive blur at that, reducible to the remembered absence of a hunger that, now, dominates all else. Israel's murmuring shows its teeth in a single obsessive thought, voiced as a demand: 'Food at once!' All else is forgotten.

What does Moses do? He tries to restore perspective. Invoking God's help in the past, he induces the people to trust in future interventions, too. He calls to mind, for himself and for them, the name God revealed to him at the burning bush, 'I am, I am *here*' (3.14). Pointing to Aaron and himself, about to be lynched by the mob, he asks, 'Who are we?' (16.7). Moses is in God's hand what the staff is in his own: an instrument, ineffective in itself, dependent on the power of the Lord. Moses makes it clear what is really going on: 'Your murmurings', he says, 'are not against us but against the Lord' (16.8). He attempts to draw the people out from their blindness, to shift their attention from rumbling tummies to the Lord's promise.

At first God seems to acquiesce in Israel's demands. He summons the whole congregation and says, through Moses: 'I have heard the murmurings of the people of Israel; say to them, "At twilight you shall eat flesh, and in the morning you shall be filled with bread; then you shall know that I am the Lord your God"' (16.12). The promise is fulfilled. Quails cover the camp that night. Next morning there is manna.

Are we to conclude that murmuring, for being undignified, does in fact work? At Massah, murmuring made God make bitter water sweet. In the desert, it called forth solid food. At Meribah it will cause God to call water forth from a rock. So can we force God's hand if only we complain long and loudly enough?

For an engagement with this question, we must turn to later parts of the Pentateuch, where God reflects the murmuring of Israel back to them. It makes for sobering reading. At the outset of the exodus, God does indeed treat Israel like children, but in order to help them grow to adult stature as covenant partners. This maturing fails to occur. Murmuring goes on, even after the giving of the Law, even when the people have set eyes on Canaan. The Lord at that point has had enough: 'How long shall this wicked congregation murmur against me?' (Numbers 14.27). Murmuring isn't innocent. It corrupts the heart, makes it 'wicked'. Murmurers, says God, are unfit to enter the land towards which they are bound. They must perish in the wilderness.

Murmuring renders the Israelites' other efforts fruitless. Why? Because it spells 'faithlessness' (Numbers 14.33); and a person without faith, a selfish person of but earthly vision, unable to pour out his or her life in trust, is unequipped to live in the land of promise. The 40 years of Israel's continued wandering in the desert were an intended exclusion from Canaan, a time of waiting for the murmurers to die, so that a new generation might rise up with an aptitude for hope, for wanting what God wants them to want.

Murmuring betrays an urge to stay in control. We murmur when we don't get what we think we deserve; when what we think of as our needs are not met. God, meanwhile, would train us for gratuity and confidence. If he lets us go through lean times, it may be to prepare us to receive gratefully some new food he is getting ready. By murmuring we decline. We crave satisfaction at once. We effectively say, 'I know best, give me what I desire, then leave me alone.' We cut God off. We exclude ourselves from the land. We condemn ourselves to die in a barren wilderness. A habit of murmuring in daily life can slowly but surely strangle a soul.

In the Old Testament, murmuring is principally linked with Israel's three first rebellions in the desert. Demanding food and drink, the people displayed their lack of trust in God's saving power. Frustration was channelled into anger against the man appointed as their leader. They murmured 'against Moses'. Moses knew he was inadequate; he had protested that from the moment he was called. He had come to accept, though, that God had made him a providential tool. Indeed, his weakness may have had something to do with his election: because Moses was no imposing leader, not strong in appearance, it would be evident to all that whatever his hand did was wrought, in reality, by the hand of the Lord.

In Egypt, Israel accepted this. On these terms they set out on their journey. Yet hunger and thirst showed the limit of their confidence. Faced with discomfort, their aptitude for abandonment turned out to be feeble. Their murmuring gave voice to a 'faithlessness' whose echo resounds through the Psalms and prophetic books. 'They murmured in their tents', we read in Psalm 105.25, 'and did not obey the voice of the Lord'. We see again that one who murmurs asserts prerogatives, which tend to be prerogatives of victimhood. Feeling hard done by, he considers himself dispensed from a committed covenantal response. Unprepared to encounter either God or other people (for encounters require openness), he stays put in his tent, nursing feelings of anger, self-pity and grudge. It is not a happy prospect.

In the New Testament, murmuring takes a different form, no less revealing. We might consider its manifestations in the Synoptics first, then in the Fourth Gospel.

Matthew mentions murmuring only once, but in a prominent place – in the last parable Jesus tells before going into Jerusalem: the story of the householder hiring labourers (20.1-16). The employer goes out in the morning and agrees with his workers on a denarius in wage. He takes others on at the third, sixth, ninth and eleventh hour, saying simply, 'I will give you what is right.' At the end of the day, each gets the same salary, irrespective of the hours put in.

'Now when the first came, they thought they would receive more; but each of them also received a denarius. And on receiving it they murmured against the householder' (v. 10). As they are promptly reminded, there has been no injustice. The contract was scrupulously kept. The first-comers murmur, not because they have received too little, but because they think their companions have received too much too easily. The object of the murmuring is the householder's kindness.

Murmuring is a protest against grace. Not for nothing does Jesus go straight on to predict that the Son of Man will be given up, mocked, scourged and crucified (20.18-19). The gift he has come to bestow is more than murmuring men and women can abide; they will feel compelled to eliminate the giver, clutching their sense of privilege and precedence, not wanting to be put on a par with late arrivals whom they deem unworthy of their deserts, their company.

This theme, which Matthew refers to Christ's teaching, recurs in the Gospel of Luke as observational reporting. There are three incidents of murmuring in Luke, all revealing a similar motivation. In chapter 5, at the outset of Christ's ministry, the 'Pharisees and scribes murmured against [Jesus'] disciples, saying, "Why do you eat with tax collectors and sinners?"' (5.30). The Twelve plus One are perceived as a whole. What offends is their collective overstepping of boundaries. They claim to be men of faith, yet mingle with people excluded from devout circles. Establishmentarians are upset, and murmur. They worry that this openness to disreputable people will be seen as a way of condoning unhealthy lifestyles and choices, compromising Israel's law. This attitude can easily occur in any religious context, ours not excluded. We want to draw a line between those who are in and those who are out, taking it for granted, of course, that we're in.

Jesus' life and teaching are based on a different perspective. Again and again, he makes the point that we are all, in fact, outsiders, yet welcome in through God's free, efficacious gift. On this account, the Good News is perceived by many pious believers as bad, even dangerous news. It muddies the waters. It brings others too close for comfort. It obliterates their sense of being special and secure. Murmuring gives voice to the right-thinking view that the unrighteous should kindly be kept out. Jesus answers sharply: 'I have not come to call the righteous' (5.32).

The scene is repeated in Luke 15. Jesus, by this point a well-established preacher, draws surprising crowds. 'The tax collectors and sinners were all drawing near to hear him. And the Pharisees and scribes murmured, saying, "This man receives sinners and eats with them"' (15.2). Apart from all else, this kind of attitude is tedious. Murmuring betrays, again, immaturity. Murmurers want to be affirmed. For that, they require the condemnation of others. A dynamic of displacement is intrinsic to murmuring, a pointing of the finger at others, away from oneself. Jesus answers with the parable of the lost sheep, revealing God's purpose to restore each man, each woman, to communion with him, and so with one another. If this divine design makes us murmur, we have not come far in putting on the mind of Christ.

The third Lucan reference passes from the general to the particular. It is about Zacchaeus. When Jesus entered his home, '*all* murmured' (19.7). The protest was universal, as if to say: 'Outreach to the lost is well and good, but not to *him*, for God's sake!' Reading this story in private, we might replace Zacchaeus with our least favourite neighbour, and observe our own gut response.

In John's Gospel, all five incidents of murmuring occur in chapters 6 and 7, in the context of the feeding of the multitude. John's account is like an inversion of the rebellions at Massah and Meribah. There, people murmured because God did not feed them with required speed. Here, murmuring issues from feeding, as people, having eaten, refuse to take on board what has just taken place. They want bread. They want God to give it. But they do not want God to make any claims on them. At issue is not a complaint that God gives too little, but that he asks too much. He disrupts their sense of who he is, who they are.

The people 'murmured at Jesus because he said, "I am the bread which came down from heaven." They said, "Is not this Jesus, whose father and mother we know?"' (6.41f.). Murmuring here reveals another tendency to which we are prone. We want God to give us what we want; yet we want him to stay at eye-level. We want him to be a provider God while we stay in charge of our lives. That is what happened at Meribah. On the far side of Galilee, Jesus asks those who ate with him to make a further step: 'This is the bread which came down from heaven, not such as the fathers ate and died; he who eats this bread will live for ever' (6.58). It was more than they could take. People, even people close to him, murmured and walked off. It is an infinitely melancholy scene. It is possible to reject the gift of God.

The longer I live with the Rule of St Benedict, the more I study it and come to love it, the more I am convinced that the schema by which St Benedict distributes the Psalms for the various hours of the Divine Office deserves close consideration. He stresses that anyone who finds a better arrangement can apply it. But what is better? There is a theological consistency to St Benedict's schema that I have not found in any other proposal. It is worth paying attention to individual Psalms that St Benedict prescribes for set positions in the course of the day or week.

One such is Psalm 94, the Invitatory Psalm. The word 'invitatorium' does not occur in the Rule, but was early applied to this specific Psalm, which St Benedict asks to be sung 'deliberately', with a refrain, at the outset of each Vigil Office.[62] Pronouncing *invitatory* carefully, we recognize in it a familiar set of words, to do with 'invitation'. This, of course, is a notion St Benedict puts before us emphatically. In the Prologue, having orchestrated a dialogue between Christ and the soul, with the former asking, 'Who is there who yearns for life?' St Benedict exclaims: 'What, beloved brothers, could be sweeter than this voice of the Lord inviting us?'[63]

We talk of being 'invited' to a party, to a dinner, to a holiday. This is how we should conceive of monastic life. The Lord is the host who would share something good with people dear to him. Each night at Vigils his invitation is addressed to us anew.

Psalm 94 consists of two parts. The first part is full of ebullience, inviting us to make 'a joyful noise' and to 'come into [God's] presence'. The Lord, then, is close to us, at hand. We can approach him. He awaits us. The motive for praise is threefold. First, we celebrate God as creator. The depths of the earth, the heights of the mountains, the sea: all were made by his hand. And he is *our* Maker, too. The God we worship is infinitely high, yet close to us, having willed us into being and formed us to his own design. Our second reason for praising God is that he is 'our salvation'. The wound of sin is evoked with the assurance that God, by grace, has healed it. We can come before him unafraid, for he has saved us. Third, we rejoice before God because he leads us as our shepherd and guide: 'We are the people of his pasture, the sheep of his hand.' Even in the valley of darkness we know: he goes before us and stays with us.

The second part of the Psalm adopts a different perspective. It evokes our resistance to being saved. It acknowledges that much in us militates against embracing the invitatory: 'Oh that today you would listen to his voice!' The cry is impassioned. It implies that deafness to God's call is the norm, not the exception, even for believers. There follows a reference to scenarios we have considered: 'harden not your hearts, as at Meribah, as on the day of Massah, in the desert'. 'Your fathers', says the Lord, 'put me to the test, though they had seen my work.' They provoked the Lord to anger, to the point of making him swear, 'They shall never enter my rest.' The message is clear: the same could happen to us unless we, here and now, respond differently.

By means of this summons St Benedict would have us reflect each day on the vicious effect of murmuring, an attitude so at odds with all we aspire to as monks. His specific injunctions concern instantiations in daily life of the drama of Massah and Meribah. In chapter 5 he censures the murmuring of the disobedient. At issue is an unwillingness to assume the direction of another: a refusal to advance into the freedom of self-giving, as we hanker instead after fleshpots of self-will. Even one who appears to obey yet grumbles 'secretly' is debarred from Canaan.[64] His attachment to self divides his heart, and a split heart is unfit for love's covenant.

Because murmuring puts a monk's soul at risk, it must be censured. St Benedict prescribes excommunication,[65] which is simply the objective recognition of a stance assumed subjectively, the murmurer having effectively cut himself off from communion.

The chapters at the centre of the Rule, chapters concerned with daily life, show when a monk is most tempted to murmur: when he sees another receive a concession or possession denied himself;[66] when he is hungry;[67] when circumstances deny him his quota of wine;[68] when he feels too much is required of him.[69] We may recognize these occasions of trial. It is good to find them squarely acknowledged. That way, we can prepare ourselves for battle and avoid the dead end of Massah, the childish posture that dictates: 'Give me what I want *now*, or I will go no further.'

Should that voice make itself heard in our heart, let us take Psalm 94 in hand and reflect on how unworthy such bickering is of people who have pledged to follow the Lamb wherever he goes, who have accepted the Lord's call to climb his holy mountain. We have signed up for an Everest expedition, not for a casual picnic.

Alas, murmuring remains a current topic. One can still come across monks or nuns for whom complaining is a lifestyle, who grumble away, constantly seeing themselves as hard done by. Whole communities can adopt a discourse of negativity, in which conversation tends towards statements of discontent as to some magnetic field. In the words of the Psalm, such communities and monks correspond to the Lord's rebuke, 'These people do not know my ways.' This is not to say that they are given to depravity or heresy. The words must be read in the context of the exodus.

God intended to trace a straight path from Egypt to the Promised Land. But the people wouldn't follow. They were sure *their* route was better, that the Lord (and his stuttering lieutenant) had got lost. Above all, they were constantly drawn back to the place from which they had set out, idealizing what it had been like, and what they had been like within it. I think of a verse from Ecclesiastes: 'Discontent lodges in the bosom of a fool. Do not say: former times were better than these' (7.9f.).

Murmuring displays the capitulation of hope through a nursing of retrospect, a refusal to move forward. Yet our life of faith is a journey. Its destination is glorious if only we look up to behold it. May we not be like the murmurers of old who absurdly 'despised the desirable land' (Psalm 105.24).

'Come, ring out our joy to the Lord; hail the God who saves us.' This is the invitation our call holds out to us. We, too, are on a desert journey, having retired, like our twelfth-century Fathers, to a 'wilderness'. The Lord guides us still, a cloud by day, blazing fire by night. Our itinerary is set out by means of our *regula*, our Rule, which indicates the most efficient way of reaching the goal we say we desire. The Lord has called us together in this place to be an image of wandering Israel, to manifest the Church *in via*. He has given us to one another as brothers, friends, supporters, to encourage each other when the way is wearisome, to lead by good example, good zeal, good cheer.

The joy to which we are called is no temperamental accident. It is the expression of a soul that tends forward, drawn by love's yearning to see the Beloved, with a heart enlarged to embrace and contain whatever companions the Lord will give us to carry on our way. As long as our shared progress on this royal road is marked by lightness, gratitude and faith, we shall, by God's grace and shared resolve, keep the acid rain of murmuring far from our horizon.

QUEMADMODUM

We will all have had the experience of suddenly seeing the sense of a verse of Scripture as if reading it for the first time. This happened to me last Thursday, on the feast of St Laurence. I was working on my report in the monastery in which I had performed a visitation, so didn't go to Vespers in church, but recited the office from my iPad breviary. The short reading was from the end of the First Epistle of Peter. It began, '*Quemadmodum communicatis Christi passionibus, gaudete*' (4.13). The standard English translation reads, 'Insofar as you share in the sufferings of Christ, rejoice.' The Latin text sustains that sense.

However, '*quemadmodum*', the adverb introducing the passage, means literally, 'in whatever way'. We might render it like this: 'In whatever way you share in Christ's sufferings, rejoice.' It was this that made me sit up. You may think I am being too subtle: 'in so far', 'in whatever way', what difference? Both are responsible renderings of the word *katho*, which occurs in the Greek and simply means 'as'.

I ask for your indulgence as I try to expand my reflection further. We are touching the core of our Christian experience: the working out of our redemption. How is the mystery of Christ made effective in my life? This is the question this passage raises, a question on which our discipleship turns.

To contemplate Christ crucified and say I should rejoice 'insofar as I share in his sufferings' is to place the Saviour's redemptive pain in a category apart, as something towards which I must rise, something elevated above normal experience, defined by qualitative difference. This perspective stresses the sublimity of Christ's sacrifice. It springs from a reverential attitude that is noble and good.

The risk is that it sanitizes redemption. It suggests that only pain that is somehow pure, or perceived as such, is worthy of association with Jesus' pain. If we are not careful, we end up making a distinction between 'virtuous' and 'common' pain, the first being the only currency worthy to be counted. Thereby, self-righteousness lurks at the soul's gate.

We may have met devout people who, whenever they feel slighted, sigh resignedly: 'I offer it up in union with Christ's passion!' We may ourselves sigh like that from time to time. By all means, let's throw whatever straw we carry into the furnace of Christ's love. Yet let's be wary of counting ourselves co-redeemers. Let's be wary of thinking that our *exalted* pain, which may be just a bit of wounded pride, is somehow worthy of Jesus' cross in a way that the pain of common sinners isn't. Let's be wary of thinking, even implicitly, that others need to *be* redeemed while we contribute to redemption. By raising the sufferings of Christ upon a pedestal, we have the satisfaction of rising with it – though this illusory ascent in reality amounts to a fall.

Let's consider the other meaning of St Peter's statement, in terms of the *'quemadmodum'* as I read it the other night. To attend to 'whatever way in which we share in Christ's suffering' opens the field up a great deal. It invites us to take a fresh look at what Christ suffered, and how.

Permit me to share a remembrance that has shaped me. Twenty years ago, I visited Venice with a friend. We went round the city's sights. We set aside a morning for the Scuola Grande di San Rocco, home to a magnificent cycle of paintings by Tintoretto, a master of the Venetian *cinquecento*. What we had planned as a cultural outing became a spiritual experience. The centrepiece of Tintoretto's composition is an immense account, 12.5 × 5.5 metres, of Christ's crucifixion. I studied this famous picture with admiration, though as time began to pass, I was even more struck by what I saw in my friend. Transfixed by the scene, he stood in a corner, looking terribly sad, terribly alone. I knew better than to disturb him. I withdrew, and waited.

After a long time he came out. We silently made our way through the remainder of the *scuola*, then lunched. The meal, too, was silent. Concerned, I asked, 'What's wrong?' I can't remember what my friend said, but I'll never forget what he had seen: the frightful squalor of it all!

At the centre of the painting is the Saviour's cross illumined by a radiance issuing from Christ's body, a still point of upward focus. Round about is utter chaos. The Lord's Mother is there, swooning in a heap of mourning women, but the holy huddle is dwarfed by the presence of gawpers, barterers, violent, unconcerned men, some mounted on horses, taking the spectacle in as entertainment. 'You know,' my friend said, 'it probably was like that.'

I have meditated on that observation, and on Tintoretto's painting, for two decades. I think my friend was right. The solitary, nobly carved crucifixes on which, normally, we fix our attention render little of the cruelty, mess, noise and ugliness of the actual event. The darkness shrouding the land at the sixth hour was an inadequate symbol of the darkness in the heart of those who looked upon Christ's agony with cool indifference, even with scorn.

Yet for these he died. To 'share in Christ's suffering' is not to enter some rarefied spiritual experience. It is to be plunged into what the Fathers called the *mysterium iniquitatis*, the reality of sin. Christ, the infinitely fair, became man to bear this sin. It disfigured him. And he says to us: 'Follow me.' 'Do likewise.' Those are hard sayings. They are also wonderful invitations. If we embrace them, they have power to transform reality and our living of it. For 'in whatever way' sin and evil may impinge on us, we can channel the darkness into Christ's saving light, and whatever that light shines on 'becomes light' – we have it on apostolic authority (Ephesians 5.13).

The sin that clings so closely to our bodies, minds and souls, that seems at times to cripple us; the sin that surrounds us and mars our world; the 'wages of sin', sickness, diminishment and death: all this is potentially part of Christ's redemptive pain, if we, members of his body, assume it freely and bear it in his name. It is when we do just that, St Peter proclaims, that we've reason to rejoice. We do not rejoice in the suffering itself, nor in iniquity, God forbid. We rejoice because we are thereby given the grace to play a tiny share in the victory of goodness over evil. We rejoice because we are graced to let Christ's presence spread into a world that knows him not, has no time for him, and tends merely to laugh at the gift of his love, as the onlookers do in Tintoretto's picture. We rejoice in a God who cares to save uncaring mankind.

These days, there are voices in the Church that rise in predictable choruses of denunciation. They delight in decrying the decadence of manners, the breakdown of morals, the frittering away of faith. The Church has a duty to tell right from wrong, by all means. Its words should be 'Yes, yes' or 'No, no'. But above all the Church must follow in the footsteps of its Master. It is a moot point whether our times are really so much more depraved than Palestine under Pontius Pilate. Yet nowhere do we hear Jesus upbraid his Father: 'Why must I be incarnate in the midst of *this*?'

Little of the Lord's time was spent on wrathful diatribes. What he did was to assure those with ears to hear, eyes to see, that sin need never have the final word; that its wounds can be healed, its incentive forgiven. He offered comfort and transformative friendship. When no one would hear him any more, when all *he* heard was 'Crucify!', he simply carried. He stands before us in this divine mysterious silence of his in the figure of a Lamb. May we never forget that it is this Lamb we are called to follow, wherever he goes (cf. Revelation 14.4). And let us be mindful that 'in whatever form' sin assails us, the Lamb can conquer still, if we let him, and that in his victory is joy.

3. Jacopo Robusti, known as Tintoretto, *The Crucifixion* (1565), detail.

THE INCANDESCENT CORE

I have been mulling over a prayer we prayed at Mass for the solemnity of Our Lady's Assumption, at the Offertory. It goes like this:

> May this oblation, our tribute of homage, rise up to you, O Lord, and, through the intercession of the Most Blessed Virgin Mary, whom you assumed into heaven, may our hearts, aflame with the fire of love, constantly long for you.

You may ask what is special about it. Its formulae are generic, recurring at other times, in other places. This is true, but that day, while presiding at Mass, my heart stopped at the words, 'aflame with the fire of love'. I thought, 'What am I letting myself in for?' Am I minded to hand my heart over to the flame of God's love, for it to burn away anything that is not God?

The stakes were made clear to me there, at the altar, by something I had read the same morning, in an anthology of early monastic writings. In his preface, the editor speaks of images the Fathers use to describe the monk's endeavour: true philosophy, a return to Eden, the angelic life, etc. These images, he remarks, 'reveal with different nuances and accents the one and same incandescent core that animates the life of monks'.[70]

I love the word 'incandescent'. It has made its way from Latin into many European languages. 'Candescent' comes from 'candidus', meaning 'white'. The preposition 'in' charges it with intensity. As a verb it means to glow white-hot; in other words, to emit light as a result of being heated.

In the context of what animates the monk's heart, the image was luminous. When I let it shine upon my mediocre life, I felt sadness. I am called to be fire; we all are. Each must account for himself; I don't presume to speak for anyone else. But as for me, I often let myself be drawn far away from the heat-source of God's love, sometimes by indolence, sometimes by distraction, sometimes by a fatigue that contains and spreads the deadly seed of discouragement.

Such thoughts were on my mind in the early hours of the morning, as I was doing my reading and asking myself: do I even know what it *is* for my life to have an incandescent core? Then, four hours later, the Church put these immense words into my mouth: 'may [my heart], aflame with the fire of love, constantly long for you'. Who would have dared to make up such a prayer? Yet there it is, an intention that mirrors God's will for us: 'Set us on fire!' It is at once consoling and terrifying.

Our God is a consuming fire. Scripture tells us that by way of proposition. More forcefully, it shows us what this proposition means in a series of accounts of epiphanies. God appears as fire to both Abraham and Moses in crucial revelations. Divine fire is repeatedly evoked in the Psalms, as in Psalm 17, where 'flashes of fire' herald the Lord's descent to save his servant in distress. To approach this fire of presence, to stand before it, is to be caught up in its flame.

The paradigmatic example is Moses. Descending from Sinai the second time, having asked to see the Lord, he was aglow with glory. 'You shall see my back,' the Lord had declared, 'but my face shall not be seen' (Exodus 33.23). Yet after this encounter, Moses was not merely radiant. He shone in such a way that the Israelites could not bear the sight of him. They needed a screen between themselves and the brightness, as we would if we tried to gaze directly at the sun.

The veil Moses wore on his face is evoked in a passage from 2 Corinthians we regularly hear at Vespers: 'But we all, with unveiled face beholding as in a mirror the glory of the Lord, are changed into the same image from glory to glory' (3.18). Why, how, can we endure what the most outstanding of the faithful of old could not?

It is not because God's fiery glory has somehow been attenuated: it is eternal, unchangeable. Nor has our natural tolerance increased: we're as earthbound as ever we were, owl-like in the ease with which we make our habitat in darkness. What has changed in the wake of the Lord's incarnation is our capacity for transformation. In assuming our nature, the eternal Word revived a potential petrified since Adam's fall. Humanity was readjusted to divine reality, equipped to transcend nature's bounds, to rise to an intensity of being that depends utterly on divine grace.

It hasn't become more natural to behold the glory of the Lord; but we have effective access, in Christ, to what is *super*natural. We can look upon God in the measure that we have been conformed to God's image. The 'fire of love' that would blaze in our hearts as in the burning bush, the incandescence we are called to embody: these are not ours; they are not results of our performance. They are marks of God's real presence in our life, our being. We, creatures of dust, are called to glow with uncreated light. Not only are we asked to wonder at this mystery of paradox; we are invited to yearn for its fulfilment and to construct our lives in such a way that it may be fulfilled.

I stress this notion of 'construction' advisedly. We cannot induce the favour of God's presence, but it is God's declared good pleasure to bestow it. Our task is to make of our life a house in which his glory can dwell. The revelation of God's glory to Israel through Moses is followed at once by the construction of the tabernacle. There is a lesson in this for us all, an example to emulate. The Fathers were conscious of this, as we see from a passage in Cassian:

> A monk's whole attention should be fixed on one point, the rise and circle of all his thoughts be vigorously restricted to it, that is, to the remembrance of God. It is as with a man who would raise the vault of a rounded arch. He must constantly draw a line round from its exact centre, and in accordance with the sure standard it gives discover by the laws of building all the evenness and roundness required. But if anyone tries to finish it without establishing its centre, whatever his ability, it is impossible for him to keep the circumference even, without making mistakes. He cannot find out just by looking how much he has taken off by his error from the beauty of real roundness.[71]

I find comfort in these words. They remind us that there is a rational way of responding to a call that, seen in isolation, is so high it threatens to appal us, or leave us discouraged by the thought of our ineptitude. What matters is to establish, once for all, the centre of our life. If we make sure it is God, and keep checking that that centre doesn't shift, we can build our sanctuary around it.

A few days ago, I had a chat with one of the brethren in front of our new letter slots, assembled as an elegant piece of furniture by Br Andrew. Full of admiration, the brother said, 'What craftsmanship!' We recognize it when we see it: integrity of form, beauty of appearance, correspondence to purpose. All constituent parts form a harmonious, seemingly necessary whole.

In the case of our pigeonholes, this is so because Br Andrew, before he started building, had a precise idea of what he was going to make. He planned his work, worked out his measurements, made sure he had materials and tools to hand. Then he began. We build our spiritual life in the same way. There, too, we need a method, a plan and apparatus. The monastic life provides us with everything we need. What we have to do is to ensure we have stamina to keep at our task, ever refocusing our work on its fixed and living centre, God's presence. By virtue of staying close to this fire, our life will acquire, with time, the properties of fire. Our heart will flare up. We shall then be resolute in dismissing temptations that distract us from this purpose. We shall have confidence that God, who loved us first, will teach us how to love. And we shall give ourselves no rest until we have built a worthy temple for the Lord, a house both inviting and beautiful, each for himself and all of us together.

BEAR ONE ANOTHER'S BURDENS

A fundamental principle of Christian living is set out in the last chapter of St Paul's letter to the Galatians: 'Bear one another's burdens, and so fulfil the law of Christ' (6.2). It is not cited verbatim in the Rule, but is constantly presupposed, as when St Benedict enjoins that we must bear 'with the greatest patience one another's weaknesses of body or behaviour' or that 'the sick must be patiently borne with'.[72]

In both instances, the injunction to 'bear' is linked to 'patience'. In Latin, *patientia* derives from *patior*, 'I suffer', which is likewise the root of *passio*. St Benedict stresses this semantic link at the end of the Prologue, when he says that by our 'patience' we share in the 'passion' of Christ.[73] He reminds us that life in Christ has its share of pain, and that it cannot be otherwise. To be conformed to Christ is to be part of his work of redemption, fulfilled through the cross, not just as historical memory, but as living reality, as a way of being in the world.

To be members of Christ, and so, as Paul would say, to be members of one another, is to form a *patient* fellowship in every sense of the term. It is to shoulder Christ's yoke and to assume the weight of it. Though it may, from afar, seem likely to crush us, the reality is different. For if Christ charges us to bear one another, he himself bears us. And so we find, astonishingly, that a load that at first appeared to be beyond our strength is in fact bearable; that, through Christ's grace, it is not only light, but joyful, graced.

A powerful account of what it might mean to live like this is given in a classic text from Christian antiquity, the *Life of Maria, Niece of Abraham*.[74] Maria was an orphan who, at seven, was entrusted to her uncle, the monk Abraham. The abba took her in. The two lived in a double hermitage, with a window between their cells. Abraham taught Maria to love and serve the Lord, to pray the Psalter, to keep vigil.

Maria made great progress in virtue. Abraham, who loved her dearly, 'prayed for her all the time with tears', rejoicing to see her grow up to be a great, humble, charitable Christian. The two lived this way for 20 years. Then, disaster struck. A certain depraved fellow, 'a monk by name only', would come to visit Abraham on the pretext of seeking counsel. In reality he was on fire with lust for Maria.

Over a year, he used his visits to seduce the young woman with sweet words. Maria, unprepared, gullible in her virtue, was readily deceived. One night she climbed out of her window to meet her admirer. She found no tender embrace. The false monk violated her, then ran off, leaving Maria in unspeakable despair.

So appalled was she by what had happened 'that she beat her face with her hands, wishing she were dead'. Mortified by the shame she had brought down on her uncle, she was tempted by the demon of despair. She thought there could be no way back to her life of devotion. What other ways were open to her? Only one: she got up, fled to the city, changed her appearance, and gave herself over to a brothel.

All this happened secretly, of course, but Abraham was warned in a dream. The form of that dream speaks volumes. What Abraham saw was a huge, foul snake come hissing towards Maria's cell, where it snatched a dove and swallowed it, crushing the bird in its jaws. Waking up to find his niece gone, he was distraught. From that day, he 'prayed constantly day and night for her to the Lord'. After two years, he could bear the unknowing no longer. He called on a well-connected friend in the world to make enquiries – which is as close as any Desert Father has come to hiring a private detective. The man found Maria. He saw what she was doing. He so grieved for Abraham he hardly had the heart to tell him the news.

Abraham, though, was unshaken. Losing no time on melodramatic display, he braced himself for action. Without hesitation, this son of the desert, a recluse for years, asked his friend to procure him a horse and a soldier's dress. He took with him a pound's weight of coins, and set off to the brothel where Maria worked.

Posing as a customer, Abraham sweet-talked the madam, who promised him a pleasurable night. Poor Maria thought her uncle, disguised, was just another lascivious old man. Yet when he approached her, she thought she 'smelt the sweet smell of asceticism'. It brought back memories of innocence and gladness, making her distress sharper still. Only when the two were alone behind locked doors, did Abraham make himself known.

He did not speak a word of reproach. On the contrary, his heart overflowed with compassion. This is how he put it into words:

> What happened, my dear? Who hurt you, my daughter? Why, when you sinned, did you not come and speak of it to me? For of course I would have done penance for you. Why did you not do that? Why instead did you hurt me, and give me this weight of grief? For who is without sin, save God alone?

Maria, we are told, 'sat like a stone', overcome by shame and fear. When Abraham asked her to come back with him, she protested: 'How can I pray again to God when I am defiled with sin as filthy as this!' Abraham was adamant: 'Upon me be your sin, Maria, and let God lay it to my account. My dear, do not draw back from the mercy of God. If sparks could set fire to the ocean, then indeed your sins could defile the purity of God!' Consoled at last, Maria knelt at Abraham's feet and wept hot tears, saying, 'What can I give you, O Lord, to repay all that you have done for me?'

For having read this story many times, I am always extremely moved by it – moved, and troubled. For even as Abraham became to Maria a sign and dependable proof of God's redemption, bearing her disgrace as his own, so am I, and so are you, called to bear our share, in union with the Lamb of God, of the world's sin. We are to practise this bearing in community, prompt to shoulder whatever weighs down our brother. Our charity must not be confined to pretty words. It must be patiently embodied.

This carrying task has two complementary aspects. St Paul, in Galatians, at once qualifies his first injunction, 'Bear each other's burdens', with another: 'Let each carry his own load' (6.5). Is this not a contradiction? No, it is not, as we can see from our story.

Not for a moment does Maria blame anyone other than herself. A case could be made for casting her in the role of a victim. She refuses that role. She does not blame life or circumstance, not even the wicked 'false monk'. She acknowledges, 'This is what my life has become', and owns the truth of it. Thereby her load of grief is somehow set free. It can be shared, borne, and, yes, 'taken away'. The sin, the pain that sticks to us, is that for which we blame others. Such sin remains glued to our soul by the adhesive of resentment. To experience our burden as light, we must rise above its heaviness. Then, if we let him, Christ raises us up, unmediated, by himself, and through the members of his Church, our brethren.

To be dandled on God's knee (Isaiah 66.12), to become again a child of God, I must first freely assume the weight of being me. On this paradox our progress to maturity depends. Recently, an old friend sent me her latest book, about parenthood. In it, she observes:

> Most of us live with painful experiences from our childhood. They get the better of us only if we lock ourselves within them, seeing them as an excuse for our inadequacies through life. We must move on. [...] We will not become adult until we learn no longer to blame our parents.[75]

These are words from another register, but they express, I think, the sense of St Paul's imperative: I must assume responsibility for what I have become, whatever, whoever, has played a role in making me that way. Only then am I free to be carried and freed. Only then am I fit to take my share in carrying others – and so to find my place in a communion of charity that is the closest we get, here and now, to the splendour of the kingdom of heaven.

FOLLOW THE WAY MARKED OUT TO THE END

Last week we prayed, with the whole Order, for a nun of the abbey of Maria Frieden in Germany, Sr Maria Donata Offermann, who went to the Lord on 25 February, 91 years old, after 58 years of monastic life. The community's obituary tells us that

> Sr M Donata was a very dear sister, who every day in her final years peeled a large bucket of potatoes,

prepared vegetables, cleared away the breakfast things – all this with enthusiasm – while she ever harboured a single thought: 'Jesus and Mary!'

A thoroughly monastic tribute. We recognize the synthesis of mystical aspiration and humble service. Had this been all we knew about Sr Donata, we might have thought no more of it. We would simply have recited a prayer for the repose of her soul, giving thanks to God that yet another faithful life has run its course within our Cistercian communion.

Sr Donata's itinerary turns out, however, to have been anything but ordinary. She was the fifth of six children born to a farming family near Bonn, and trained as a nurse. She exercised this profession for several years until, aged 32, she entered Maria Frieden. We sense something of her spirited character when the obituarist remarks: 'To the sisters' astonishment, she waltzed in wearing high-heeled shoes – and turned into a hard-working, dependable Trappistine nun.'

Sr Donata made her first procession on 15 August. The solemnity of the Assumption would always remain dear to her. But she was not to live long in its ambiance of lightness and joy. 'In 1965 she succumbed to a psychiatric illness from which she never really recovered.' She entered a Night of Faith and experienced deep darkness of soul until just after the beginning of the new millennium. That is more than 35 years!

The more I think of this fact, the greater is my reverence for our Sister Donata, whose name means 'Given'. She, who arrived at the abbey so lively, with such elegance, was to be entombed in spirit for decades. We can only begin to imagine what she suffered. We can sense, I think, the heroic determination that lay at the root of her fidelity. And we catch a glimpse of what went on in her heart of hearts when we are told of her vestment-making work.

Her main job was to 'create embroideries after her own patterns. Later she turned to decorating borders with exquisite needlecraft illuminations. She lived in a world of colours and flowers. Her signature was a couple of marigolds somewhere in the picture.' There is poetry and beauty in this description. There is, too, a tremendous testimony of faith. Deprived of light within, of the subjective experience of faith, Sr Donata focused her best attention on a liturgical art that represents our religion's solidly objective character: the embellishment of vestments worn for the celebration of the Sacred Mysteries, which are present, real and effective whether or not they are recognized as such.

Even here, she quietly withdrew to the 'borders' – in search of an environment suited to the colours and beauty she had known and lost awhile, but was certain, in faith, of finding again.

Her hope was vindicated.

During the fifteen last years of her life, her joy in faith returned with such fervour that she declared to all and sundry: 'This place is heaven on earth! I am just an old dolt, but Jesus and Mary are within me, and I see them in you as well. I really see them!', at which she would point straight at the person before her.

The final years of Sr Donata were marked by illness. A hip operation left her crippled. Colon cancer raged to claim her for itself. She increasingly developed dementia.

Her radiance was undiminished. The sisters describe how she would

> sit for hours in our freezing cloister, before a life-size crucifix, with an enormous rosary in her hand, praying it countless times. She greeted with joy anyone who happened to walk past. The pictures she painted as substitutes for needlework when her strength diminished, she generously gave away as gifts.

The photograph that accompanies the obituary shows our sister looking, indeed, radiant, as if bursting with joy, over a bucket of potatoes. Her smile, I dare say, must have been contagious. A fall down a flight of stairs immobilized her during the final weeks of her life. She died peacefully on Sunday 25 February, the day on which our Gospel proclaimed Christ's transfiguration on Tabor.

I was all the more struck by the example of Sr Donata since I had just finished the latest book by Nicolas Diat, *Un temps pour mourir*, with the subtitle, 'The last days of the lives of monks' ('*Derniers jours de la vie des moines*').[76] The book, made up of testimonies from eight monasteries of how a number of monks have left this life, may seem a lugubrious read. Its message, though, is inspiring. At a time when death is anaesthetized and driven out of sight, Diat shows its dignity, even its beauty, especially when it comes as the crowning of a life given over to the search for God, with the promise of vision and fulfilment.

One of Diat's chapters is dedicated to the monastery of En Calcat. It is a reflection of its abbot, Dom David Tardif d'Hamonville, that resonated within me when

I read the notice from Maria Frieden. One death the abbot recounts is that of a monk who, after years of monastic life, entered deep depression and withdrew into a form of spiritual autism. Dom David is emphatic, and says: 'I do not wish to brush under a carpet this reality that touches *any* monastery.'

He remarks that psychiatric illness can be a closed door sealed with 'No Entry' signs. He speaks of the trial of monks on whom such darkness descends, for whom the things of God lose all attraction, whose contact with others is curtailed by an inability to share what they are living through – which may seem to them to spell the failure of a spiritual vocation.

While I admire the abbot's frankness in touching this matter, his account left me dissatisfied, being too much restricted to the natural realm.

That illness affecting the mind can have a spiritual dimension is something we, here, have witnessed close at hand. It is also what shines wonderfully through in the life of Sr Donata. Thirty-five years of desolation in the framework of contemplative life is a burden beyond the strength of most to bear. Her stamina must have been exceptional. But what stature she reached by living faithfully; what light poured out of the darkness it was given her to plumb! Remember the words that distilled her mature experience: 'Here is heaven on earth!' When we touch the working of grace in the life of another, we must exercise reverential caution. We must be careful not to over-spiritualize. We must be no less careful not to leave the action of God out of the equation. How often what seems to us happenstance, or even great misfortune, turns out to provide occasions for God's providence to work. We must look out, in ourselves and in others, for the call inherent in the way our lives turn out in fact, even though we might have planned them differently.

In a reading from Jeremiah this week, we heard these wonderful words: 'Listen to my voice, then I will be your God [...]. Follow right to the end the way that I mark out for you, and you will prosper' (7.23). It must have been a temptation for Sr Donata to take another path when the one she had entered upon led through such barren, fearful territories. However, she kept walking, right to the end. She kept her eyes fixed on a light that, eclipsed without, was only perceptible within, in her soul's unseeing desire. And she trusted the reality of that desire, all the while leaving behind a trail of the delightful flowers and colours that were missing from her interior landscape. Her fidelity bore fruit, and so she is to the Church a noble and prophetic figure, a guide for us, her brothers, on our vocational journey.

4. Sister Maria Donata Offermann.

TO LET THE BODY BREATHE

In 2009, Hungarian TV broadcast a documentary entitled *Confessors and Traitors* about Hungary's Catholic Church under communism. When Mátyás Rákosi seized power in 1945, the Church was subject to persecution. It brought forth confessors and martyrs. The integrity of faith was kept alive in small pockets of believers, often driven underground, while the institutional Church was gradually brought to heel by an atheist government. Through a mixture of incentives and threats, seminaries and monasteries were infiltrated. Episcopal sees were filled with loyalists reporting to the state. Fear did its work, as did ambition and indolence. By 1989, when communist rule ceased, Hungary's Church was compromised. How badly, no one knew: many were tempted to resist retrospect, to look ahead, to let bygones be bygones. *Confessors and Traitors* insists that this is not an option. In the film, Asztrik Várszegi, Archabbot of Pannonhalma, calls for determined engagement with the past, 'the way a watercourse must be cleared of obstructions to permit new impetus and flow'. Only thus, he goes on, 'can trust in the Church be restored. We cannot preach the Gospel truly until we are again found trust*worthy*.'

An analogous challenge faces the Church as a whole as we strive to come to terms with a harrowing catalogue of misconduct and abuse. It is not only a matter of bringing individual cases to justice. It is a matter of seeking healing for the ecclesial body, which has carried this legacy as a pollutant for far too long. People are calling for action, for heads on platters. The prevailing sentiment, understandably, is one of anger. Anger,

141

prudently channelled, can serve righteousness. But it can also blind. I perceive a certain dull-sightedness in much that is said about celibacy.

Celibacy is widely considered to be at the root of the problem. There are those who think it an impossible requirement, a dehumanizing regimen that will naturally repel those of sound inclinations and attract others whose intimate lives are troubled. We should be wary of such assumptions. They are at odds with many luminous examples of joyful, integral, fruitful celibate lives: I hope every Catholic has known some such. Further, there is the risk that we unwittingly adopt prevailing secular notions of sexuality and sexual pathology, forgetting that celibacy pertains to the order of grace.

Grace builds on nature, by all means. Any vocational discernment must first ascertain if sufficient aptitude exists for consecration in freedom. It is irresponsible to let someone undertake a sacred commitment he or she does not have the resources to keep. Yet it would be wrong to see celibacy just as a function of natural disposition. I wonder, indeed, whether we have not come to take it too much for granted, as part of the package of priestly or religious life?

In the early Church, it was viewed as a sign of the *eschaton*. In his treatise *On the Incarnation*, St Athanasius adduces chastity as proof of Christ's power to restore human nature in a way unthinkable without divine intervention: 'Who has destroyed the passions in men's souls to the point of rendering fornicators chaste, [...] to give courage to those held in the grip of fear?' 'Who', he goes on, 'has considered that virginity is not an impossible virtue for man?' Only Christ![77]

To vow oneself to this virtue is an immense, heroic proposition. I fear we have often failed to make our seminarians and novices ready for it.

How are men and women best assisted to prepare for celibacy? Not chiefly by classes, though these can help. The crucial thing is to help them develop the courage to face the deepest strands of their being and to put these into words. Before I joined the monastery, a monk told me: 'The monastic life is unbearable if you do not have someone to whom you can say absolutely everything.' I can confirm the truth of that claim.

We must be able to speak humbly, frankly even, about our desires, to work out what they mean, to direct them in healthy ways. Monastic tradition offers a wealth of lived wisdom. The Fathers recorded long disquisitions on *porneia*, or lust. We may be surprised at their preparedness to call a spade a spade, to name the twistedness of wayward impulses. We will be no less struck by their stress on the potentially Godward orientation of our desires, recoverable by grace. 'Everything', says St John Climacus,

> is possible for the believer. I have watched impure souls mad for physical love but turning what they know of such love into a reason for penance and transferring the same capacity for love to the Lord. I have watched them master fear so as to drive themselves unsparingly towards the love of God.[78]

Anyone tempted to dismiss this statement as cheap sublimation might read it in context and discover that Climacus had few illusions about sinful humanity's potential for perversion. What he helps us realize is that 'perversion' and 'conversion' are cognate nouns. If we believe we are created in God's image, that this image extends even to embodied desire, the direction and hallowing of desire becomes a key ascetic task, with the potential to open our whole being to the transforming power of grace. We should not be naïve. But neither should we lose hope. What matters is to be truthful.

Sr Emmanuelle of Cairo, commonly regarded as a saint for her long ministry among ragpickers, wrote her autobiography for posthumous publication. It came out just after her death in 2008, at three weeks short of a hundred. Sr Emmanuelle voices her conviction that, 'When the naked truth of a human life is told, God is revealed between the lines.' She is unsparing with herself and speaks openly, not least about her struggles with celibacy. She relates an experience that occurred when she was well into middle age, a seasoned religious: 'From head to toe my body was live embers.' It was more than she could bear. She could not pray. She could not think. She did not know what to do.

At last she went to see an old nun. 'I put my burning hands into her cool hands and murmured, "I can't do this any more, I'm worn out." I raised my downbeat eyes towards hers. They had the translucency of a wellspring. I felt myself reborn to innocence.' Their dialogue was brief and essential. The old nun *knew*. She said, 'You're being tried by fire. That's good for a religious. Fire purifies metal, and tests it.' The remedies she proposed were simple. 'We shall seek together. You must pray, but act, too. Help yourself, and heaven will help. Now you see only your difficulty. Open your heart to the hurt of others, and your own wound will be healed.' Sr Emmanuelle refers to this trial as a turning point in her life of discipleship. But what would have happened had she tried to keep the fire under a lid?[79]

Neither John Climacus nor Sr Emmanuelle provide blueprints. But they set standards to which we should dare to aspire. A standard, first of all, of honesty and fidelity, of readiness to seek help, to struggle, to trust grace, to believe that holiness is possible; a standard, too, of conversation. How many priests and religious speak with their bishop, superior or director at this level? How many bishops, superiors or directors would be prepared for such an exchange? To become trust*worthy*, we must learn to entrust ourselves. No structural reform can do that for us. No amount of cerebral training can heal the heart's wound, only the experience of being fully known. If we would clear the watercourse of grace in the Church, it is not enough to stop the occurrence of abuse – though this is paramount. The body needs to be purified and re-oxygenized. Decades after writing *On the Incarnation*, St Athanasius composed his best-known work, the *Life of Anthony*. Anthony of Egypt, the founder of monasticism, lived to be 105. Each day he would say to himself, 'Today I begin.' He summed up his spiritual testament to his brethren in the words, 'Let Christ be the air you breathe.' Those are words of life, to live by.

5. Having assumed her own vulnerability, Sr Emmanuelle was free to greet others with open arms.

THE FINAL NOTE IS JOY

Earlier this week, someone sent me a quotation from Friedrich von Hügel's *Letters to a Niece*. Von Hügel, you will remember, was a notable Catholic intellectual, an articulate proponent of the modernist movement. Austrian by birth, a baron of the Holy Roman Empire, he was at home in many European countries and languages. He settled in his wife's native England. When he died in 1925, he was buried at Downside. The passage I read evokes the mature state of soul of this complex man deeply familiar with the Church's spiritual patrimony, whose principal work is entitled, *The Mystical Element of Religion*. He wrote this:

> Religion has never made me happy: it is no use shutting your eyes to the fact that the deeper you

go, the more alone you find yourself. [...] Religion has never made me comfy. I have been in the deserts ten years. All deepened life is deepened suffering, deepened dreariness, deepened joy. Suffering and joy. The final note of religion is joy.[80]

The baron's experience is certainly not unique. How might we respond? What would you say to someone who presented you with this kind of outlook in confession?

The first thing I would say is that, yes, certainly, it is futile to pursue religion as a means to happiness – even as it is futile to pursue it as a means to anything else. If there is truth in religion (and you and I have staked our lives on there being such truth, an absolute, infinitely desirable truth), it is an end in itself. To instrumentalize it will be frustrating and destructive. To find faith is to face the depths, yes, and the depths are never comfortable. I think von Hügel is right in saying that deepened life spells deepened suffering that matures into deepened joy. I am less sure about 'deepened dreariness'. Dreariness is monotony, and whatever else the life of the religious seeker might be, it is not dull. Provided we remain engaged in the search, deeply committed to it, we shall be in movement, in a state of becoming.

What are we to make of von Hügel's distinction between happiness and joy? Theologically, joy is a fruit of the Holy Spirit. It is a gift to be 'earnestly desired' (1 Corinthians 12.31), to be pursued (in the sense St Benedict exhorts us to 'pursue peace'[81]), even to be conquered. Happiness pertains to human experience. It cannot be induced, but it can be received. It is not incompatible with a lucid perception of the pain and limitations of life. Happiness, it seems to me, is intimately tied up with gratitude. It springs from an increasingly acute sense of not deserving the good things given me, yet seeing them poured out upon me nonetheless. If we enter this logic of gratuity and make a generous response, a kind of blessedness cannot but be ours.

This is at the heart of a Psalm verse that has always been central to monks, inasmuch as it sums up the life we construct together: 'How good and how pleasant it is when brothers live in unity' (Psalm 132.1). We must never lose the pleasantness of community life out of sight, never stop aspiring to it or weary of building it up. The secret is to be ready to seek and find it in the most ordinary things. Is it not happiness I feel on hearing a crisp bell call me to prayer in the first light of morning; on having a simple supper of cold milk and warm bread after a tiring day's work; on finding myself carried by the goodness and fidelity of my brethren; on realizing, in a flash, here and there, what it is to be a member of the Church, Christ's body?

There is a tendency in the peculiarly Western spirituality in which von Hügel was steeped that glorifies darkness, overemphasizing the misery that is simply part and parcel of our pilgrimage in this vale of tears. The Fathers of the East have always, I'd say with reason, regarded this trend with suspicion. They stress that the nature of God is light, that the closer we draw to God, the more we, too, are illumined by that Light which the Church in one of its most ancient hymns calls 'gladdening'. To keep the yearning for the light alive, then; to move actively towards it; to see, with spiritual sight, that it shines even in darkness; and to await its dawn gladly, with thanks: this is the Christian calling. If we admit as much, must we not say that the pursuit of that high goal is happiness? With each passing year, I am more convinced that it is. Every morning, when I pray the *De profundis* for the dead, I reflect on the words, '*Magis quam custodes auroram*' (Psalm 129.6f.). Greater, much greater, than the watchman's yearning for dawn is my expectation that the Lord's salvation will be manifest in me and around me, that I shall know the Lord's outstretched arm.

Tomorrow, at Mass on the First Sunday of Advent, we shall sing the glorious introit, *Ad te levavi*. It sets the first verse of Psalm 24: 'To you have I lifted up my soul: My God, I trust in you. I shall not be put to shame, nor shall my enemies laugh at me: not one of those who wait for you will be put to shame.' So important is this verse to the liturgy of the day that the Church sets it twice, first in the introit, as a stately eighth-mode piece, then in the offertory, in the more interior modulations of the second mode. What is it to 'lift up' my soul? Above all, to look up and out, to relinquish introspection and to see myself as created and redeemed with infinite tenderness, called to an ever-increasing intensity of life. 'My God, I trust in you,' says the Psalmist. To trust is to entrust oneself, to seek in God the assurance we can't find in ourselves. Trust is the basic attitude of the believer. It underpins and enables faith. For who believes a message, or a man, he doesn't count trustworthy?

This approach puts von Hügel in perspective. Created as we are in the image and likeness of God, upliftedness-of-soul is actually connatural to us. We struggle to know this natural state, for our ability to know God spontaneously has been wounded by the Fall. Were we, God forbid, to be stuck in a state of mortal sin, this knowledge could be effectively obliterated, for we do have that awful capacity: to put the life of God in us to death. Still, if we let grace work and cooperate with it, we can be certain, in faith, that God raises up what is fallen, accepts the oblation of our service, grants forgiveness of our sins and admits us to fellowship with the flock of those he has chosen. You will recognize here the intentions from the prayer *Hanc igitur* of the Roman Canon of the Mass, which precedes the *Epiclesis*, when the priest calls down the Holy Spirit on the gifts of bread and wine.

In the liturgy the mystery of faith is made manifest and palpable. With St John we can say, truly, that we, too, bear witness to that 'which we have heard, which we have seen with our eyes, which we have looked upon and touched with our hands, concerning the word of life' (1 John 1.1). As we enter upon Advent, we might aim to rediscover the riches put before us in the Church's liturgy and sacramental dispensation, a source of grace blessedly objective. Provided we are well disposed, this source wells forth living water whether we feel it or not. It renews our lives in the image of our Saviour and lets us take our share in the work of the world's redemption.

For God became man, let us not forget it, to save. The extreme measure of the incarnation would not have been taken had it not been vital. The world needs salvation now as much as ever. The Lord is coming to save *us*. He calls us to rise up to receive him and so to know the transfiguration of the world's pain through the mercy of Christ Jesus. By his gift of himself, darkness is irradiated with light. Suffering is swallowed up in joy. The happiness we seek finds its glorious fulfilment in beatitude.

PART TWO

A MONASTIC YEAR

4

SEASONS

ADVENT

Micah 5.1-4:
And they shall dwell secure.

Hebrews 10.5-10:
Lo, I have come to do thy will, O God.

Luke 1.39-45:
*Blessed is she who believed that the
Lord's promise would be fulfilled.*

Since the century of Charlemagne, the Latin Church has
spent the last week of Advent invoking Christ under a
series of invocations that urge him to come quickly. We
know them as 'O Antiphons' on account of their initial,
exclamatory O. Today we call out: *O Key of David!* What
does it mean? The answer lies in the twenty-second chapter
of Isaiah. There, we find the city of David, Jerusalem, in
turmoil. It is at war, surrounded by enemy forces. This
crisis is a God-sent scourge. By means of it, the Lord would
call the people 'to weeping and mourning, to baldness and
girding with sackcloth'. So what do they do? They indulge
in an orgy of oblivion. Supposing there'll be no tomorrow,
they break down their houses to fortify the ramparts for
a day or two. They slay their livestock, roast meat, pour

the wine that remains and chant: 'Let us eat and drink, for tomorrow we die.' There is no trace of joy in such merriment, charged with the dark energy of despair. A besieged city acting like that has lost hope. Its feasting is a mockery of fate, a burp in the face of the gods.

Blamed for the breakdown of morale is the city's steward Shebna. His name is synonymous with vanity. While the nation collapsed round him, Shebna made monuments to himself: a carved tomb; a splendid habitation. He thought he could buy immortality for money. He thought his status would make him immune to existential threat. Not so. Isaiah reveals his future: 'The Lord will hurl you away, O strong man. He will seize hold of you, whirl you round and round, and throw you like a ball into a wide land.' I am citing from the *Revised Standard Version*. The Hebrew is more graphic. The word rendered 'ball' sustains the meaning 'dumpling'. So much for Shebna's airs! The Lord will pick him up like a handful of dough, squeeze him into a lump, then – plop! – out he goes through the kitchen window. His place will be taken by another, one worthy of the steward's robe and girdle. This man, Eliakim, will be 'a father to the inhabitants of Jerusalem'. He will care for them, take charge of their welfare. 'And I will place on his shoulder', the oracle continues, 'the key of the house of David; he shall open, and none shall shut; he shall shut, and none shall open.' O *Key of David!*

The Jerusalemites feasted as they did because they thought themselves caught in a trap. They couldn't conceive of a way out. Into this despair, God sends hope. He assures them that there is in fact a key, a key that both opens and shuts. There is no deadlock. There's potentially a future. But will they want it? Will we? Our world is in many ways like beleaguered Jerusalem.

When we look at the wars and epidemics raging, at the movement of peoples, at climate change, at the state of the Church, can't we also feel tempted to draw the blinds, pour another drink, and wait for it to end?

As Christians we must resist such moral surrender. There is no state of affairs so arrested that the Key of David can't unlock it. It is a master key in the absolute sense. 'Come', we sing in today's antiphon 'and lead forth the captive from prison, come and release those who sit in darkness and the shadow of death.' That holds for every prison, every darkness, every death, even the most intimate. There *is* an exit.

Our readings this Sunday provide examples of God's intervention in apparently hopeless situations. The Gospel portrays the embrace of two women great with child: one elderly, thought to be barren, the other a virgin. Who would have thought? The prophet Micah, a contemporary of Isaiah, affirms that the lost sons of Israel, seemingly lost to hope, will come back; they who are fearful now 'shall dwell secure'. A 'new' ruler, whose origin is 'of old', will make it happen. Again, who would have thought?! The greatest paradox, though, is contained in our reading from Hebrews. It speaks daring words, placed in our Saviour's mouth when he 'came into this world'. His task was to renew creation, destroy death and forgive sins. What sort of vast dispensation would that require, what armies of angels?

Let us listen again to Christ declaring the arms he takes up for this battle: 'A body thou hast prepared for me. Then I said, Lo, I have come to do thy will, O God!' This is the key that opens and none can shut, shuts and none can open: a complete abandonment to God's saving will and a firm resolve to put it into practice in the body, in the concrete reality of life. It is Israel's key, Mary's key, the key of Christ, the Son of David. It is potentially our key, too, yours and mine. Christmas is not, in essence, a cosy affair. It presents us with an offer of new life, new resolution. It calls on us to make a choice. Will we let the key of obedience and faith turn in *our* creaking locks? If we do, what joy, what freedom we shall know – what peace! He whom we await 'is our peace'. Why waste time and effort seeking it anywhere or in anyone else?

CHRISTMAS VIGIL

Isaiah 9.1-7:
They rejoice before these as with joy at the harvest.

Titus 2.11-14:
Awaiting our blessed hope, the appearing of the glory of our great God.

Luke 2.1-14:
There was no place for them.

The very setting of this Mass is a symbol. We are gathered in the compact enclosure of the night that seems to cover all things like a blanket. From within the darkness, we rejoice in the spark God has lighted through the birth of the Messiah. One looking in from outside might think it an inconsequential light. What is this flicker against the expanse of the night? Only if we have known total darkness, a darkness seeming to swallow all light, pregnant with hopelessness, can we know the exultation a tiny spark of light can bring. Why does light affect us so? Why do we so long for it? Light tells us we are not alone. It proclaims that our solitude need not be final. At Christmas we celebrate God's shining in darkness. We greet that light as a person with a name. He is Emmanuel, 'God with us'. He is Jesus, 'God saves'. He comes to be, to abide, with us.

Isaiah foretold the gladness of those on whom this light has shined. 'Thou hast multiplied the nation, thou hast increased its joy; they rejoice before thee as with joy at the harvest.' It is a classic image. But do we, in fact, know the joy it speaks of? Not many people now harvest food they need for subsistence. We may grow herbs on our windowsill, cabbages in an allotment. But they are not what we live on. For that, we go to Morrison's. We have largely lost a sense of the land as that from which we draw life. Is that not why we treat it so cruelly? The land was barren at the beginning of creation. Then God showered it with goodness, brought it to fruition, made it yield of its abundance. 'And God called the dry land earth.' We know it now: earth can easily revert to 'dry land', vulnerable once again to floods of water.

These lessons from ecology are part of Christmas. For one and a half thousand years, the Latin Church has expressed its longing for Christ in Advent through a pair of moving refrains: 'Drop down, heavens, dew from above, let the clouds rain down the just one; let the earth be opened and bring forth a Saviour' (Isaiah 45.8). God comes to us like mild spring rain, like dewfall. Are our lives 'earth', porous, open, hospitable, fit to yield fruit? Or are they 'dry land', hard, unreceptive, apt to let grace wash over them with no chance of entering in? Mary, the Mother of God, is our model of openness. Her 'Yes' was unconditional. She was totally generous, so free. She can seem distant, though. Can her calling impinge on ours? Yes it can. Let me give you an example.

Five days ago a monk died in the abbey of Mount Melleray. He was called Fr Celestine. He was unremarkable in many respects. He never held important positions. He had the sort of jobs no one notices. For long years he was assistant infirmarian. He loved that job and performed it with devotion. When I knew him, he was already advanced in dementia. He told me many times of his family, his pond, the statue of Our Lady he once had bought from a shop in Cork. But we never really talked. He taught me wonderful lessons nonetheless. His light-blue eyes had a clarity that cast light. His face in repose was a smile. During endless walks round the cloister, he would stop passing monks and tell them: 'Jesus loves you!'

Some months ago, I turned up at Mount Melleray in mid-morning. Fr Celestine was in the refectory, waiting for something to happen. In front of him lay a banana, his favourite fruit. I went to greet him. He looked at me first with bewilderment, having forgotten who I was. Then he beamed, picked up his banana, presented it, and said: 'Have this!'

One of his last utterances, before he lost speech, was to the brother who cared for him. At bedtime one night, Fr Celestine fixed him and said: 'I know who you are!' Then he fell silent.

He was fruit-bearing soil, ploughed by fidelity, irrigated by the constant, deliberate practice of kindness. All his life, he had let waters of grace pour in. They had worked their quiet transformation. How will we respond when our rational defences drop? Faced with a stranger, will we clutch our banana and growl? Or will we offer it in a gesture of connatural hospitality? Will the love of Jesus be our lasting certainty? Will we wish those around us to know that they are known to us – and dear? What sort of soul will we have forged for ourselves?

Christmas is not a date in the calendar. It is a state of being. The clouds do rain down the just one. If only the earth received him, instead of surrendering to desertification, the Son of God would enter our lives, make them productive and glorious. When we open our hearts to him with gratitude, rejoicing at the harvest, the Christmas miracle continues. Light shines in darkness. The heavenly choirs sing. Just be still and listen.

CHRISTMAS DAY

Isaiah 52.7-10:
Eye to eye they see the return of the Lord to Zion.

Hebrews 1.1-6:
*He reflects the glory of God and bears
the very stamp of his nature.*

John 1.1-18:
*He came to his own domain and his own
did not accept him.*

'He came to his own domain', says St John, 'and his own did not accept him.' In what way was the world to which Christ came his 'domain'? The title does not indicate merely generic sovereignty over creation, as if, like a feudal lord normally resident abroad, he arrived one day to claim territorial rights. The bond between him and our world is much, much tighter. The Word that became flesh, let's not forget, was in the beginning; through him all things came to be, not one thing had its being but through him.

That each existent thing has a history of complex origin is something we take for granted. As post-Darwinians we know about the potential adaptation of species to environments. In geological finds, we handle wonderful imprints of ancient forms of life on fossils resembling lacework in stone. Not only do we trace the development of species; our ability to crack, at least partly, the code of DNA has shown us the span of individual uniqueness, each of us displaying an unrepeated pattern. However many billions of people might walk this earth of beauty and pain, there will only ever be one of *you*. Your mark is no one else's to make.

To get our minds around this immensity is hard enough. To envisage it as issuing from a single mind is almost scary. Yet this is our firmly held, thoroughly reasonable belief: that each earthly manifestation of creative exuberance originates in God's eternal Word; that this Word, by whose design our physical being exists, has a correspondingly exhaustive view of our heart; that, though he knows us through and through as we are, he loves us; that he would grant us a share in his eternal life; that he took flesh of the Virgin Mary, poured himself out under Pontius Pilate, and continues to give himself for us now, present in the Church, in the saints, in the sacraments; that he has left his fingerprint on all that exists. Everything potentially speaks to us of the Word. Do we live attentively enough to behold the world with contemplative wonder, conscious of the gift it represents, its barely concealed glory?

The poet Elizabeth Barrett Browning, best known for occasionally melancholy love poetry, was a writer of metaphysical depth with flashes of insight we might call mystical. In the seventh book of *Aurora Leigh*, she speaks of the 'twofold manner' of everything around us. Each thing is fully itself, yet at the same time a symbol of something else. As for us, human beings, we live in strange kinship with all. Why are we moved, she wonders, by the elegant shape of a leaf, a lovely stone? Birds aren't, nor is a horse 'before a quarry a-graze'. The answer must be that there is a correspondence between our minds and the mind that made the universe. And what is the pulsation of biological life if not a yearning for eternity? 'Glancing on my own thin veinèd wrist', says the poet, 'in such a little tremor of blood / The whole strong clamour of a vehement soul / Doth utter itself distinct.' She goes on to exclaim:

Earth's crammed with heaven,
And every common bush afire with God;
But only he who sees, takes off his shoes,
The rest sit round it and pluck blackberries,
And daub their natural faces unaware
More and more from the first similitude.[82]

At Christmas, God does not only show us who he is; he reveals us to ourselves. He shows us that we live, move, have our being in a sacramental world. The Word incarnate asks us to re-read everything, existence as such, through the lens of his self-revelation. To do this, we don't have to be great scholars. It suffices to be fully alive, to have a pure heart, a longing soul, and, above all, keen eyes.

'Only he who sees, takes off his shoes.' To think that God, Emmanuel, is truly in our midst, and we see him not! To think that the deepest truth about ourselves, 'the first similitude', is God's own likeness, lost awhile, yet now, by virtue of Christ's birth, restored, if only we choose to be remodelled by it, abandoning the search for instant satisfactions – our blackberrying – in order to put on a new humanity, our faces, cleansed of disfiguring stains, once again fit to reflect Christ's luminous face. Today, in an explosion of confidence born of God's gift, we ask for nothing less. In the Collect, the Church lets us pray 'that we may share in the divinity of Christ, who humbled himself to share in our humanity'. For this, Christ was born, lived and taught, suffered, died, and rose again.

EPIPHANY

Isaiah 60.1-6:
Arise, shine out Jerusalem, for your light has come.

Ephesians 3.2-3, 5-6:
*I have been entrusted by God with
the grace he meant for you.*

Matthew 2.1-12:
We saw his star as it rose.

The story that frames today's feast tells of the magi who, following the star, arrive from afar to pay homage to the newborn Christ. They represent the 'gentiles': all peoples of non-Jewish descent, who, for being outside the line of Israel's election, are called to inherit God's promise. The magi stand for all of us who, by grace, have been grafted into the Abrahamic covenant. We are hardly any longer conscious of what this means, having got used to thinking of ourselves as naturally chosen and called. We take God's gift for granted, so the magi have lost their significance. They are reduced to being ornamental flunkies around our cribs, purveyors of oriental mystery. Our ancestors in the faith were differently minded. Conscious of being latecomers to the banquet, they saw the wise men as prototypes and needed intercessors. Lovely stories were spun around them. They were endowed with royal dignity, splendidly named Balthasar, Melchior and Caspar. Their origin was variously traced to Arabia or India. From the sixth century, relics of the magi were venerated in Milan. They stayed there until

1164 when Frederick Barbarossa transferred them to Cologne. That is where the magi's shrine remains – worthy of rediscovery, perhaps, as a site of pilgrimage, a place to give thanks for the benefaction of faith?

For indeed, the focus of today's feast is not so much on the persons of the magi as on the grace that guided them. They could only accomplish their journey because they were prompted and led. Their faith presupposes God's faithfulness. Throughout Advent, the Church's Vespers hymn is an ancient prayer that begins with the words, *Conditor alme siderum*: 'O kind Creator of the stars, eternal light of believers!' The star guiding the magi is more than a cinematic backdrop. It bears witness that the Mover of the universe and Mary's child are one. The cosmos bears out Scripture's promise. Supernatural truth proves itself in nature. The universe is itself a book of revelation, readable by anyone with eyes to see. Emerging from this is a wonderful truth: our God is a God who wants to be known. Epiphany – the word means 'manifestation' – teaches us this. It bids us see the natural world as a catalogue of signs by which God directs us to himself.

God delights in awakening our spiritual perception. He guides our freedom with consummate discretion. Rarely does he dazzle. His patience with us is at once a gift and a mystery. In our reading from Isaiah, the prophet proclaims that the true light has come, that God's glory has risen on us. Then he makes a paradoxical affirmation: although his glory rises, 'night still covers the earth, and darkness the peoples'. Why? Why, when the light came to shine in the darkness, did it not illumine it completely, with a self-evidence that would be irresistible? Why does God, who is light, give darkness a chance?

Here and now, we can be certain of this: darkness has its part to play in the unfolding of God's saving work. Darkness, whether outward or inward, has power to hollow us out, to make us deep and so better able to embrace the gift of God in its fullness. Sometimes, when we moan about the hiddenness of God, perhaps we forget how *other* he is, what inward transformation must take place in us before we can know him. The magi's pilgrimage tells us not to expect the comfort of broad daylight in our journey of faith. The light of one star is all we need to be led where God would have us, to worship before his incarnate mercy.

This points to a further aspect of Epiphany: the call we have received to be light to one another, to live starlike lives. Isaiah's call to Jerusalem, 'Rise up and be light!', is addressed to each of us. In the Gospel, Jesus says, 'I am the light of the world.' Our relationship with him rests on that certainty. We must never, though, forget that he also says to you and me, '*You* are the light of the world.' We have our part to play in the continuing epiphany of God. How can the world believe if no one bears witness to truth? God would have us reflect his light and bear it into all kinds of darkness. Extraordinarily, though he knows our frailties and failings, he counts on us to make him known. Our lives are to be epiphanic.

In his poem *The Magi*, W. B. Yeats speaks of the 'uncontrollable mystery' that gave the wise men no peace once they'd seen it in Bethlehem's stable, 'on the bestial floor'. On this thirteenth day of Christmas, we might pray for a like restlessness, for grace to be so stirred by Christ's light that it sets us on fire, that our world's present night may become, by grace, a luminous desert vigil, aglow with innumerable stars.

The Magi

Now as at all times I can see in the mind's eye,
In their stiff, painted clothes, the pale unsatisfied ones
Appear and disappear in the blue depth of the sky
With all their ancient faces like rain-beaten stones,
And all their helms of silver hovering side by side,
And all their eyes still fixed, hoping to find once more,
Being by Calvary's turbulence unsatisfied,
The uncontrollable mystery on the bestial floor.[83]

6. William Butler Yeats at about the time of writing *The Magi*.

THE PRESENTATION OF THE LORD

Malachi 3.1-4:
The Lord will suddenly come to his temple.

Hebrews 2.14-18:
*A compassionate and trustworthy high
priest of God's religion.*

Luke 2.22-40:
When the day came for them to be purified.

168

In the time of Noah, the flood filled the earth through 40 days of unremitting rain. Forty days were required for the embalming of Jacob in Egypt, once he had drawn up his feet into his bed and expired. When Moses entered the cloud of God's presence on Sinai, he stayed enwrapped in it for 40 days. The men sent by Moses to spy out Canaan, 'to see what land it is', returned to camp after 40 days, with a cluster of grapes on a pole. Christ was tempted by Satan in the desert for 40 days. For 40 days after his resurrection he appeared to the apostles. During 40 days of single-minded devotion, the Church prepares our hearts and bodies for Easter, a Lenten pilgrimage that recalls the 40 years of Israel's journey home. Today is the fortieth day after Christmas. We also have just performed a journey, albeit a modest one, in chanting procession. By it, Jesus, born in obscurity, is revealed as light to the nations. In the liturgy, everything means something. So how does the 40-day time we are bringing to an end fit in with the general, biblical 40-day pattern?

The examples I have given refer to varied experiences. All, though, have this in common: they are times of gestation during which a word planted by the Lord grows to fruition. Each introduces a new division in sacred history. When, in the six hundredth year of Noah's life, the great deep burst forth and heaven's windows were opened, a new beginning was given to the human race, cancelling a legacy of infidelity. The revelation of the Law to Moses, too, introduced a new order of things, giving men and women a new way of walking with God. A new beginning carries special grace. It appeals to our idealism and sense of adventure. At the same time, new beginnings involve risk and concomitant anxiety. Caleb and his companions were not feeling brave when they returned from their foray into Canaan. They felt, they said, like grasshoppers, for 'the land we have gone to spy out devours its inhabitants' (Numbers 13.32). It is all very well to speak of a 'Promised Land' – but there be giants. A fresh start calls for courage. We must trust in God who calls us and who goes ahead.

The 40 days concluded today may seem tame compared to the conquest of Canaan. When we last heard of Mary's Son he lay wrapped in swaddling cloths. Today he is carried, still wrapped, perhaps, to the temple. What has he done in the meantime but eat and sleep? On the surface, that is all. This feast bids us go deeper, to enter the mystery of the slumbering child. Today, in fact, the Lord 'suddenly enters his temple', as Malachi foresaw. 'Suddenly' is the word. For who took any notice? Who expected it, except a couple of ancient eccentrics? Yet here he is, entering his house: the Lord, who, like a refiner's fire, will purify the sons of Levi so that they might make their offering 'as it should be made'. Centuries of expectation culminate in this instance. God's promise is vindicated at last. The salvation of the world is made manifest. And no one noticed.

This is what we must reflect on: the discretion of our God, who fulfils his promises without display. An *incognito* Redeemer, he is himself redeemed by a pair of pigeons, of all species of bird the most ordinary. 'He emptied himself, taking the form of a servant, becoming obedient unto death.' Thus the letter to the Philippians (2.7f.) summed up the mission of Christ some 50 years after the events we commemorate today. The perspective is unsettling. It jars with the comfort and homeliness of Christmas. Yet in this light, the Gospel tells us, we must see our Saviour even at birth. The offering of him in the temple prefigures the offering he later made of himself when, outside the city, his crucified body gave forth blood and water in an outpouring of grace that realized what previous sacrifices had foreshadowed. The sword Simeon saw would be a cruel sword, cutting deep. The enlightening light would shine alone in darkness.

Christ surrendered himself as readily to the arms of the cross as he gave himself up, still a child, to his mother's embrace. Suddenly he enters his temple, not as conqueror, but bound by our need, utterly given to his redemptive task. When we think of that task and of the load he assumed, our eyes become a fountain of tears. And yet we rejoice. For, yes, we, too, can now depart in peace. Our lives are safe in the hands of him whom, with Mary and Joseph, we offer this day at the altar, 40 days after his birth. From now on, this child is our peace. What can giants do to us? Christ does not let us down. May we never betray him! As peacefully as he is presented today, we are to present ourselves to him, boldly and without great fuss. We are to carry him, our weak yet all-powerful Lord, with us wherever we go, trusting him, entrusting ourselves to him.

ASH WEDNESDAY

Joel 2.12-18:
Between the vestibule and the altar let the ministers of the Lord weep.

2 Corinthians 5.20–6.2:
Be reconciled to God!

Matthew 6.1-6, 16-18:
Do not imitate the hypocrites.

In the natural world, nothing is more dead than ash, a substance produced by the perishing of other substances, a function of death. Nothing grows in ashes. There is no fruitfulness in them. It is only natural that many cultures use ashes as a symbol of mortality. In certain traditions of the East, the relatives of a person recently deceased cover themselves with ashes. It is a way of expressing their share in the passing of someone they love: by this death, something in themselves has died. Such associations are found in Holy Writ. Think of Job, the upright and blameless, when he lost his sons and daughters, his health and dignity. He 'sat among the ashes' (Job 2.8). He spoke no word. He sought out ashes to convey the content of his scorched soul.

Today, at the beginning of Lent, we, too, are signed with ashes. Their fugitive mark recalls our transience: 'Remember, you are dust; to dust you shall return' (Genesis 3.19). This central rite of Ash Wednesday concerns more, though, than just mindfulness of physical death. We perform it as we gather resolve to engage in a spiritual campaign. The liturgy speaks of a 'battle', of being 'armed with weapons'. Our heads are strewn with ashes as a sign of our commitment to fight. Fight what? In communion with Christ our Lord, to whose Passion and Rising we look forward, we set out to fight death and all that is of death. This may seem an outrageous claim, laughable to secular minds, yet it is the heart of our Christian call, duty and privilege.

The death we focus on today is the spiritual death we inflict on ourselves when we snuff out the divine light of grace by compromises with darkness. We confess and ask forgiveness for our half-heartedness, for our betrayals small and great. Grieving, we proclaim that our choices are not always right. We own our tendency to follow paths of self-destruction, prone as we are to be seduced by flighty pleasures, vain words, empty promises. What a wonderful thing it is that the Church provides a public rite by which we can unite in making such an intimate admission. What force there is in the symbol of ashes still, in our technocratic, post-postmodern world of self-satisfied sophistication. The ashes create a bond of solidarity between us. They make it easier for us to help each other choose the right way, to offer a word of support, an arm to lean on, when we see each other falter.

For, of course, the commitment we renew today does not concern ourselves alone. The prophet Joel inspires us with words rich in pathos: 'Between the vestibule and the altar let the priests, the ministers of the Lord, weep and say, "Spare thy people, O Lord, make not thy heritage a reproach."' This priestly intercession is a service to which all of us are called. It belongs to our baptismal covenant.

By that covenant we open our hearts to pray with tears for the Body of Christ in all its members, so many of whom suffer outrage. We ask that our compassion may fan embers of hope into a living fire, to shed light within us and about us. For we are not weeping into a dark hole, a void of silence. Our God hears. He responds. He waits to act. 'Behold, now is the acceptable time, now is the day of salvation.' If today we expose our sickness, it is because we know healing is in store. Throughout Lent, our eyes are fixed on the promise of Easter. This time is a time to prepare to pass from death to life.

LENT

Deuteronomy 26.4-10:
My father was a wandering Aramaean.

Romans 10.8-13:
The word is very near to you.

Luke 4.1-13:
Jesus was led by the Spirit through the wilderness.

Midway through the Gospel account, having named the apostles, Jesus prepares them for their task and for the hostility they will meet. 'When they bring you before rulers and authorities,' he says, 'do not be anxious how or what you are to speak; for the Holy Spirit will teach you in that very hour what you ought to say' (Luke 12.11). To be a Christian is to set oneself up to be accused, yet to be at peace, sure of having an all-powerful advocate who inspires right responses.

It is useful to know that the Semitic word for an 'accuser' is *satan*. The devil acquires that generic term as a proper name because the business of accusation and entrapment is for him constitutional, definitive of his being. The devil's work is to confound and convict, to sow seeds of falsehood and engender contradiction and, thereby, to provoke shame and despair. Let's not imagine, though, that the devil's schemes are grandiose and somehow brilliant. More often than not, he sets his snares in trivial ways. He catches us out in our small infidelities and weaknesses, making us swallow his hook unaware. Then he starts pulling in the line, gently at first, then with greater violence, laughing contemptuously at us.

Christ's confrontation with Satan at the end of his proto-Lent of 40 days has nothing of the sinister tumult of *The Exorcist*. On the face of it, the confrontation in the desert resembles an urbane, though acerbic, skirmish of two biblical scholars. The devil presents a line from Scripture (a genuine line, not a re-write), then asks Jesus to demonstrate the truth of that verse. It seems reasonable enough. It is impressive to note that Jesus, by way of reply, simply confronts the devil's quotation with another biblical passage – and leaves it at that. We encounter, here, the first important lesson of today's liturgy: even the truth, the Gospel truth, can be twisted if taken out of context. Without getting embroiled in futile argument, Christ confronts Satan's strategy with cool logic, on the principle that one truth cannot contradict another. Thereby he exposes the Father of Lies as the manipulator he is. Not to be blinded, then, by the confusion of particulars; to raise one's eyes to see the partial in the light of what is whole: this is the first stage of dealing with temptation.

Each of the devil's propositions corresponds to a genuine intention of Christ's, but in mirror image, inverting the perspective. The temptation to turn stones into bread meets its match in the feeding in the wilderness. *Here*, the devil proposes a magician's act, to turn something into what it is not; *there*, Christ multiplies the potential of something that stays fully what it is.

The temptation to rule the world corresponds to Christ's post-resurrection words, when he tells the Eleven: 'To me is given all power in heaven and on earth'. *Here*, the devil suggests a usurpation of authority; *there*, Christ assumes a kingship properly his, bestowed by the One who created all that exists in freedom, without envy.

The temptation to jump from the temple's parapet has as its counterpart Jesus' words from the cross:

175

'Father, into your hands I commend my spirit.' *Here*, the devil provokes an act of daring, to force God's hand; *there*, Jesus gives himself up to reality as it is in fact, voicing his trust that, even in the throes of dereliction, the Father's hands hold him lovingly, securely, ready to carry him through the dark waters of death.

In each of these instances, the Accuser attempts to impose a scheme of his devising, pushing God to act. Jesus, by contrast, asks only for the Father's will to be done, ready at each moment to receive what is given, in circumstances not of his making, as a graced disposition, awaiting the Father's good pleasure in what actually happens. This is how we, too, are invited to live.

'The Holy Spirit will teach you what to say,' Christ tells the disciples: how does this work out for himself when he is in the Accuser's dock? The words given him to speak are not wild charismatic utterances; they are not even new words. They are his deeply personal appropriation of words traditional and venerable. He teaches us something crucial: God has already given us everything we need to confront evil, to expose lies, to expound the truth. His inspired Word is eternal, at once ancient and new. Our task here and now, in our fast-moving hyper-modernity, is to make that Word our own: to hear it, understand it, feed on it, and assimilate it as our substance. Thereby we shall find not just nourishment for ourselves, but a measure pressed down and overflowing that we can freely share with others. We can use this Lent to re-root ourselves in God's Word. In the imagery of the ninetieth Psalm, in which today's liturgy is suffused, we can 'abide in the shade of the Almighty', there to experience freedom from the fowler's snare; to learn that God is with us to deliver us and give us his glory. His truth, if we do not resist it, will surround us like a shield.

PALM SUNDAY

Isaiah 50.4-7:
*The Lord God has opened my ear, and
I was not rebellious.*

Philippians 2.6-11:
Christ Jesus emptied himself.

Luke 19.28-40:
The Lord has need of it.

The events of the day we now call Palm Sunday unfold within a careful scenography that, in bimillennial retrospect, is astounding. In faith, we see before us God incarnate about to effect the world's redemption. We acclaim the luminous stature of the Saviour. Everything about this day is majestic, full of consequence. Yet in the middle of it all, we hear Jesus give instructions about the donkey he would use to enter Jerusalem. If you are tempted to ask, 'What could it matter?' think again. Our Lord, in the Gospel, admonishes us never to speak useless, ineffectual words. Whatever he himself says and does is significant, salvific. So we must ask what we can learn from details of this narrative, what their message is.

The donkey provides, in fact, a helpful focus for reflection. Donkeys and asses occur often in the Bible. We think of Balaam's ass, which beheld the angel that its rider didn't see (Numbers 22.22ff.); of the ass in Isaiah's prologue, which knew 'its master's crib' and so made its way into the imagery of Christmas (1.3); of the wild ass of the Psalms, a symbol of freedom, quenching its thirst from desert springs (103.11). The reference in today's drama is specific, though. It points to a verse from the prophet Zechariah (9.9), cited in the Gospels.

The context of this verse is the ousting of Israel's God-unfearing neighbours. A day of reckoning will come, says Zechariah, when kingly dignity will be restored to Zion: 'Rejoice greatly, O daughter Zion! Shout aloud, O daughter Jerusalem! Lo, your king comes to you; triumphant and victorious is he, humble and riding on an ass, on a colt, the foal of an ass.' The relevance of this motif for Palm Sunday is obvious – but we can go deeper still. For behind this text lies a more ancient, more mysterious reference that suffuses the account like the *organum* of medieval chant; a fixed note that adds depth and implicit harmony, even, at times, hints of discord.

I refer to a line from Jacob's deathbed blessing of Judah at the end of Genesis (49.10f.). The patriarch assures this lion's whelp: 'The sceptre shall not depart from Judah [...] until he shall come to whom it belongs [...]. Binding his foal to the vine, and his ass's colt to the choice vine, he washes his garments in the wine and his vesture in the blood of grapes.' Jesus is a descendant of Judah: we know that from the genealogy we read on Christmas Eve. And the cross, which today rises before our eyes, is likened by the Fathers to a winepress. They found in Isaiah 63.3 this line which, for them, foretold the crucifixion: 'I have trodden the wine press alone [...] and have stained all my raiment.'

The ass's colt Jesus took care to ride is thus a symbol with a wide range of meanings: it suggests at once a Davidic king's reconquest of Jerusalem; the fulfilment of patriarchal promise; the new wine that will flow from the sacrifice on Calvary. The time is upon us, we are meant to see, when God's purpose is about to be perfected. Veiled foreshadowings, the mystic stirrings of a few enlightened hearts, will assume embodied form. Prophecy will prove itself in history.

To read the Passion in this way is to gain rich insight. But the point I am eager to make is of a different order. It is this: that God intends us to decipher the history of our salvation thus. In realizing providence, he deliberately picks up clues he has dropped at other times, in other places. He does this to help us make sense of what is happening now. A writer or composer might work likewise, introducing, in a prologue or prelude, themes that reveal their potential only later.

God constructs his story with us as a work of art. This isn't to say that each detail of the story is lovely. The Bible is startlingly honest in naming the ugliness and grief into which our existence easily descends. To be a Christian is not to subscribe to some aestheticism whereby the world becomes a pretty place if only we put on the right contact lenses. No, we profess that we inhabit a broken, often cruel world, a world in need of saving. But what we learn from the example and teaching of the Lord is that no sin, no pain, is beyond integration into God's overarching narrative – a story of unmerited grace that extends from light's original emergence out of darkness to the everlasting praise of the Jerusalem on high.

Therefore it matters to concentrate on the language of signs by which God manifests his agency and presence even in the midst of our wilful chaos. We will discover not only a key to the reading of Scripture, but a tool for the interpretation of our lives. We will realize that God, the all-powerful, can draw meaning forth from what is in itself senseless; that he is able to turn even anger into praise, to reveal the victory of life through death. The days ahead are wonderfully rich in such lessons.

7. *Christ in the Winepress*, Meester van het Martyrium der Tienduizend (1463–7).

MAUNDY THURSDAY

Exodus 12.1-8, 11-14:
This day is to be a day of remembrance for you.

1 Corinthians 11.23-26:
Every time you eat this bread, you proclaim his death.

John 13.1-15:
Now he showed how perfect his love was.

Anyone who has tried to render a phrase from one language into another knows that translators must make choices. Rarely is it possible to reproduce the flavour of a statement with its range of associations and ambiguities. A phrase that in the source language is suggestively open may have to be nailed down in the version. A clearer, more memorable message may result, but sometimes at a cost. The liturgical version of our Maundy Thursday Gospel says of Christ at the Last Supper that, having loved his own in the world, 'he showed how perfect his love was'. Earlier translators have tended to prefer, 'he loved them to the end'. There is much to say in favour of their choice. It renders the Greek word for word; underneath it, we hear the spoken Aramaic. But what does it mean to love 'to the end'? The *quality* of love is at issue, yes. To love to the end is to love to the point of completion. We learn something of the fullness of Christ's love there and then. But the 'end' shows us, too, that the Saviour's love *endures*. Our Lord 'is love', John writes in his Epistle. That love, says his Prologue, was 'in the beginning'. This evening he tells us it remains 'to the end'.

Christ is *Alpha* and *Omega*. He is the same today, yesterday and always, the beginning and the end. Love in the beginning, love to the end. What is love? What does it mean to love? Few questions are more urgent. A poet of our times gives an answer that repays consideration. Only the lover, writes Elsa Morante, can know.

Alone the lover knows. If you love not, I pity you!
The myriad lives will seem to you then but common
and cheap
Like the sacred Host to unconsecrated eyes.
Only the lover has eyes to see the splendours of the Other,
With access to the house of twofold mystery:
The mystery of sorrow and the mystery of joy.[84]

We often hear it said: 'love is blind'. It isn't true. Infatuation is blind, like any passion. But love is not. Love sees. It is alert to what a person might become. Indeed, it generates becoming. It causes seeds to sprout. The lover, says Morante, traces splendour where another sees dirt. What is the Sacrament held high in a monstrance to unhallowed eyes? A piece of bread, no more. Likewise, if we do not love, the world we inhabit, and the lives that touch ours, seem pointless and dull. Love alone makes us capable of mystery. Love sets us free from our confinement in ourselves. It brings about communion. It gives itself and knows how to receive.

Christ loved those who were his in the world. The Twelve were his friends. He had given them all he had received from his Father. Yet he knew they would abandon him, and soon. Peter would disown him thrice. Judas had already left his heart's door open to the enemy, his purse weighed down by silver. Faced with imminent betrayal, on an evening made dark by the shadow of the cross, 'the Lord Jesus took bread. He thanked God for it and broke it, and he said, "This is my body. It is for you."' He loved them to the end. Even before it had taken place, he saw beyond their betrayal. He left them a memorial that would heal their broken hearts when he had gone forth from this world. By it he would be present in his absence.

'Do this in memory of me.' Christ speaks not only of the performance of a rite. He speaks of what it means. 'Do this', that is: pour out your life in love as I have done. Lest we think that good intentions are enough, he sets a standard we must follow. He washes our feet. The feet that turn away from him, *our* feet, betrayers' feet that stray from his commandments, are cleansed by hands our liturgy calls 'venerable' and 'holy'. The Lord claims our feet for himself, as if to say, 'one day you will come back to me'. That is what love is. That's what love does. It sees the penitent in the offender. It sees contrition in a heart of stone. It sees a shoot of tenderness in barren fields. It pardons wrong before it is committed. It gives itself into the hands of faithless folk, that is, into our hands. And says, 'Do likewise.'

Is there love in our hearts? We shall know by what our eyes see. If the myriad lives seem unworthy of attention; if we shun those in need, keep ourselves to ourselves, avert our gaze, bear resentments: then we do not love as Christ commands. If in the lives that surround us we see Christ; if the pain of others moves us to pity; if we pardon; if we wish to help and serve; if we see in every woman, every man, every child a flicker of God-given glory, then we love. Then we know. Then we shall act on what we know. 'I give you an example', says the Lord, 'that you may copy what I *do*.' Love is not content to think and feel and watch. Love risks and does, right 'to the end'.

8. Elsa Morante at her desk, trying to find the right words for what she knows.

GOOD FRIDAY

Isaiah 52.13–53.12:
Yet ours were the sufferings he bore.

Hebrews 4.14-16; 5.7-9:
We must never let go of the faith we have professed.

John 18.1–19.42:
Mine is not a kingdom of this world.

The King sleeps. At this point on Good Friday, peace descends. An overwhelming tension ceases. From the sixth hour, darkness has covered the land like the lid on a pot. The crowds have jeered, the elders mocked. At the foot of the cross, while our Saviour suffers in awesome solitude, soldiers have played games. The Eleven have watched, tormented, from a distance. A sword has pierced Christ's Mother's heart. Then, silence. When Christ yields up his Spirit, the action stops as in a screenplay, at the director's call. We kneel in reverence and confusion. We rise, and find that all is different. Our hearts are heavy still, but they are no longer rent. It is accomplished.

The Passion of John marks this contrast pointedly. Until Christ's death, the story moves forward by dialogue. Different voices are heard, interrupting, contradicting and disparaging each other. Then we're raised to see the scene from above. 'It was the day of preparation', John tells us, and serenely goes on to show how Sabbaths of old were symbols of this moment, when the King takes his repose. His six days' work is done. With infinite care he is loosed from the excruciating tree, bones still unbroken. His body is washed, anointed and perfumed, then wrapped in cool linen. A tranquil garden tomb gives him a resting place. No one speaks. What could be said? Signs suffice. Dusk falls. There is a breeze. Crickets sing.

At this point, our celebration also takes a different turn. The cross we shall shortly adore is no longer just an instrument of torture. It is a symbol of redemption. On it, we sing, 'hung the salvation of the world'. An ancient chant for Good Friday proclaims that, 'because of the wood of the tree, joy has entered the world'. On this day of supreme anguish, we sing of joy. That is what makes us Christians. We live in the conviction that death, thanks to Christ's work, has lost its sting. It is no longer compact darkness. A rose-fingered dawn can be perceived in it, even today.

The king sleeps. Shall we, then, sleep? No! We must be vigilant in prayer. We must be ready and remember: what in Christ has been accomplished is still worked out

in us. For us the Sabbath is not yet. We have to labour.
Romanos the Melodist, the great sixth-century poet-
theologian, sings, in a hymn on the crucifixion:

My soul, my soul, rise!
Why do you sleep?
The end is drawing near,
you'll be in tumult and confusion.
Therefore recover your senses
so that Christ our God may save you,
he who everywhere is everything's fulfilment.[85]

These lines are echoed in a tremendous statement of
Pascal's: 'Christ will be in agony until the world ends. We
shouldn't sleep during that time.'[86] What Pascal means is
not that Jesus is a captive of the cross. Golgotha is locked
in time. It can't return. Christ, once risen, will not die again.
Death has no power over him. Yet it is true to say that his
agony persists. What Christ has done must be assumed by
us, his members. We have *our* cross to bear, *our* night to
penetrate. *Our* eyes shall see, and not another's.

Our crosses, for the most part, are unspectacular: the
wages of sin, paid out time and again; pain in illness;
pain in relationships; failing faculties; the thought
of death. We are daily reminded, though, that ours
are hostile times. Each day, Christ's call to 'follow' is
enacted in the lives of men and women who, like him,
are despised, rejected and put to death for his sake. We
might remember one such.

Fr Frans van der Lugt was a Jesuit priest who for
50 years served in Syria. His base was Homs, the Old
City, which for three years has been under rebel siege.
Some weeks ago an armistice allowed some Christians to

escape what had become a death-trap. I wrote to a friend, another Jesuit, to ask if Fr Frans was safe? He replied:

> Fr Frans has chosen not to leave. Not only is he pastor of the Christians who have nowhere else to go; he has become the shepherd, too, of many others. Even men we tend to fear have found in him a father, one who breathes on them a spirit of charity and peace. He is a great man. What he has done and continues to do will forever remain a luminous point in the night of our anguish.

Twenty-three days later, Fr Frans was dragged out of his house and shot – not, I stress, by 'Islam' as a generic category, but by an individual for whom this priest's adherence to the cross was a scandal.

Golgotha is past, yet continues. Fr Frans shows us what discipleship can involve. He died as he had lived: peaceful, loving, forgiving. His gift of himself will bear fruit, we can be sure. When we bend low to kiss the cross, let us remember what we undertake. We pledge to live and die with Christ, to forgive and to be reconciled. We leave bitterness behind. We resolve to die to sin. If we're sincere, the cross will vanquish now as it did then. What today makes us weep will, three days from now, fill us with gladness.

EASTER VIGIL

Genesis 1.1–2.2:
God saw all he had made, and indeed it was very good.

Romans 6.3-11:
*Consider yourselves to be dead to sin but alive
to God in Christ Jesus.*

Matthew 28.1-10:
There is no need for you to be afraid.

This night, the Church not only exults in the victory of Christ. It shows us how his victory crowns a long process of development. The rising of Jesus is an astonishing event, but it is no surprise. The Lord has carefully prepared it. We find it foretold 'in Moses and the Prophets'. When Cleopas and his friend, dragging their feet towards Emmaus, met the Lord, he told them 'the things in all the scriptures concerning himself' (Luke 24.27). In this Vigil, he does the same for us. The readings we have heard show the Lord to have been constantly at work among his people. He follows them always, a cloud by day, a pillar of fire by night, even when he goes unnoticed.

A trend in Western piety has tended to insinuate that God had left his people almost to their own devices until Christ came. It portrays him as an angry God, with Christ coming, at last, as a pure lamb of sacrifice sent to propitiate his wrath. Expositors of this trend like to speak of Adam's guilt. He, Adam, stands condemned before us: a renegade we'd sooner disown than claim as our father. But can this be so? In the light of what we know about God, would he condemn the work of his hands, the apple of his eye, made 'in the image of himself'? Happily, the theology of wrath is not the only voice we hear, even here in Western Europe, where we are rather obsessed with apportioning degrees of guilt.

In the late twelfth century, a different view appears, more authentic and more ancient. We find it set in stone over the north porch of the cathedral of Chartres. There, in a sculpture of great beauty, we see Christ and Adam meeting: creature and Creator, the fallen and the One who raises up. Adam kneels by Christ's feet. His head rests on the Saviour's knee. Christ, with his right hand, supports that head; with his left hand, he caresses it. His face, looking down, surrounded by a cross-imprinted halo, is solemn yet mild. One would not have thought that stone could express such tenderness. There is no violence in this encounter, only peace. The two, estranged awhile, are resting in each other, relieved, serene, contemplative. The mysterious bond between Adam and Christ that St Paul expounds for us is made visible at Chartres. Each has waited for the other. Each has suffered. Each has longed.

The twelfth-century sculptor harks back to a venerable tradition. Among its most authoritative witnesses is a third-century Syriac treatise called *The Cave of Treasures*. Though virtually unread today, many a Father of the Church knew it by heart. The treatise is a midrash, theology in story form, and interprets the destiny of Adam. It speaks of the glory in which he and Eve, his wife, were clothed before they fell. It speaks of their friendship with God, of God's *joy* in them, of the unselfconscious grace that marked life in Eden. It speaks of the grief God knew when they refused to believe that what he asked of them was for their own good. They knew better, they thought, so they trespassed. Their eyes were opened. They saw what in truth they were: mere dust, stripped of glory. The God who, until then, had been their friend became a menace in their eyes. They fled. They hid. When found, they could not look on him. They did not beg his pardon. They could not, therefore, remain in the garden of trust. They exiled themselves to a desert of thistles and thorns. The God who shuts the gate behind them, however, is not a wrathful God. He is a Father who grieves, whose maternal heart prompts him to console even as he sanctions. This is how, in the *Cave of Treasures*, God takes leave of his child:

> Grieve not, Adam, on account of leaving Paradise for judgement's sake, for I shall lead you back to your inheritance. See how I have loved you! For because of you I've cursed the ground while preserving you from the curse. [...] Since you have transgressed my commandment: yes, leave, but do not grieve overmuch. In the fullness of time I have fixed for you as an exile in the land of curses, I shall send my Son. He will descend to save you.[87]

Thus Adam and Eve went forth from Eden 'clothed in mercy'.[88] Adam, having forfeited his glorious robe, is nonetheless warmed and sheltered by the Father's loving-kindness. The Master of Chartres saw that mercy and portrayed it. There's nothing fanciful about it. What else is the sense of the chronicle of saving events, of promises of grace that, this night, we have read? How great, how faithful is God's love! How amazingly that love is attested and sealed in Christ's Pasch!

May we never forget: the robe of mercy with which we are clothed is fitted to each one of us particularly. Our God does not abandon us, nor does he play games. He longs for our return, and would have us, too, rest our head on his knee. Christ has come, seen and conquered. Our salvation is accomplished. The door to Paradise is open once again, inviting us to enter and give thanks with rejoicing.

9. Detail from Chartres, showing Adam's relief at being, at last, called home from exile.

EASTER DAY

Acts 10.34, 37-43:
To him all the prophets bear witness.

Colossians 3.1-4:
Look for the things that are in heaven.

John 20.1-9:
Simon Peter went right into the tomb.

The first text put before us on Easter Morning is in some ways a surprising choice. We might have expected something more thunderous than the account of Peter's visit to Cornelius, the God-fearing centurion who lived just off the plain of Sharon. Their exchange seems too ordinary, the sort of conversation any parish priest has had scores of times with people knocking on his door seeking instruction. We need to probe a little to realize what an *extra*ordinary account it is; why it has a vital message to proclaim on this day, which defines our identity as Christians.

Remember, first of all, who it is who expounds the Gospel of Jesus with such calm authority. Liturgically, we last encountered Peter on Good Friday, in the court of the high priest's palace. We saw him fearful, doubting of a sudden all he had been through in the company of Jesus, to the point of publicly denying him, not just once, but three times. It is a sad business to denounce a friend – and what pain we feel if we hear someone we thought of as a friend say of us, 'I do not know him.'

The stakes are raised in the circumstances, given *who* Peter thought Jesus was, given Jesus' need for companionship, even simple acknowledgement. Yet in the darkness of that night, illumined only by a smoky charcoal fire, no voice of reason or faith could steel Peter's resolve. It took the crowing of a cock to pierce his heart. It recalled Christ's prediction of betrayal. Cockcrow remains to this day the symbol of dead consciences revived. The Peter we saw then was a man in a heap. Yet here he is, before Cornelius, an officer of the state that crucified Christ, proclaiming: 'I can witness to all [Jesus] did.' We should not fall into the trap of assuming that the apostles' hearts and minds were less complex than ours. What Scripture puts before us is the account of a life transformed, of cowardice changed into courage, of doubt become certainty. How can this be?

When Peter says he is a witness to Jesus' resurrection, he does not only guarantee the truth of Christ's rising – though that statement is itself momentous. What lends force to his words is his assurance of the fact that Jesus, who was dead, is alive and exerts a transformative influence beyond constraints of time and space. The world is forever changed as a result. Peter's life is changed. Your life, too, he tells Cornelius (and us), can be changed. Peter speaks of this otherness in terms of 'forgiveness of sin'. It isn't a straightforward phrase. We all know the reality of sin. We practise it, alas, only too regularly. But sin, in the New Testament, means more than the effects of sinful acts. Forgiveness is not reducible to settling accounts. In apostolic preaching, sin is referred to as a 'power'. Sin stands for an attraction that, tragically, pulls us away from the pursuit, and attainment, of happiness.

The Greek word for sin is derived from a verb that belongs in the vocabulary of archery. It means 'to miss the mark'. To live 'in sin' is to have lost one's focus on life's true goal; to long deeply for something, yet be unfit to reach the object of one's longing. That is why the experience of sin is akin to a sense of being trapped in contradiction. Any person alert to his or her soul knows what this estrangement is like, but many now lack words to speak of it. We Christians are blessed to have the vocabulary, provided we use it as we should. To receive forgiveness of sins is to be relieved of a burden of guilt – but it is more: it is to have our lives realigned to God's call; to know a freedom so profound it is something like a foretaste of beatitude; to be healed of inner divisions and so to stand, at last, as integral, whole, and *one*. When our life is integral, our speech will likewise have integrity. That's what we pick up in Peter's conversation with Cornelius. He has become the Rock he was meant to be and stands now unwavering, dependable, a true foundation.

It is infinitely comforting to recall Jesus' patience with Peter. The Lord saw from the outset the potential in the

man, but before it could be realized, great work had to
be done: a work of acquiring faith, of abandoning self,
of learning to live in service and trust. To walk in Jesus'
company, to hear Jesus' words, could take Peter a fair bit
of the way. But for the process of change to be complete,
he needed more: the power of Christ's resurrection to
heal, reorient, and justify his life. To say, 'Christ is risen
from the dead' is to speak of something that took place
under Pontius Pilate; it is also to speak of my own life
here and now, a life renewed. George Herbert wrote in
an Easter poem:

Rise heart; thy Lord is risen. Sing his praise
                    Without delays;
Who takes thee by the hand, that thou likewise
                    With him mayst rise:
That, as his death calcinèd thee to dust,
His life may make thee gold, and much more, just.[89]

Those are words to take to heart and make our own as
we rejoice that Christ lives; rejoice, too, that we, through
his rising, have been made fully alive.

ASCENSION DAY

Acts 1.1-11:
Why are you standing here looking into the sky?

Hebrews 9.24-28; 10.19-23:
He could appear in the presence of God on our behalf.

Luke 24.46-53:
*They worshipped him and went back to
Jerusalem full of joy.*

Almost forty-seven years have passed since man first landed on the moon. In mid-afternoon on 16 July 1969 a spacecraft named *Apollo 11* was launched from the Kennedy Space Centre, entering earth's orbit after 12 minutes. Three days later, *Apollo 11* passed behind the moon and entered the lunar orbit. On 21 July, at around the time when Cistercians rise for Vigils, the astronomer Neil Armstrong opened the spacecraft's door and set foot – the first man in history to do so – on the surface of the moon. In a thoughtful phrase, he remarked that his small step was 'a giant leap for humankind'. The mission, which has left its mark on our consciousness, was a glorious triumph of science. For our theological imagination it was a disaster.

It especially confused our notions of the feast we keep today. 'Now, as he blessed them he withdrew from them and was carried up to heaven.' For us who live in the wake of the 1969 lunar mission, it is almost impossible to read those words without seeing before our mind's eye the image of the *Apollo* rocket fired off from Camp Kennedy. If we stay within the logic of the image, we are faced with massive conundrums. If Christ took off from earth in that sort of way, where did he go? Is heaven a place out there beyond the galaxies, a place we might reach by our own endeavours one day, given adequate technical know-how? Or was Jesus transported straight to the Father's bosom? If so, divine realities being immaterial, was he transformed from a person with a body to a purely spiritual being in mid-air?

You may think I'm trying to be funny. I am not. Too often have I seen and heard the Ascension represented on the basis of like assumptions. These evoke associations that are plainly absurd. I dare say that is why many people, good Christians, do not know what to think about the Ascension. It seems too much like a cartoon solemnity, a feast one can't take seriously, an occasion when faith requires more than is really *reasonable*.

In the light of this, we had better look closely at the evidence. We are well placed to do so. Uniquely, Scripture gives us two accounts of the event by the same author. St Luke tells us he was not himself an eyewitness to the life of Christ, but he carefully interviewed eyewitnesses. He collated their testimonies authoritatively in a clear narrative that grew in subtlety as, little by little, he came to understand his sources better. The account I just cited ('as he blessed them ... he was carried up to heaven') comes from his earliest text, his Gospel. It is interesting to compare it with his later account in that Gospel's sequel, the Acts of the Apostles. We heard the passage read as today's first reading. There we were told that, with the apostles looking on, Jesus 'was lifted up, and a cloud took him out of their sight'. No longer is it suggested that the Lord shot into the firmament. No, 'a cloud took him'.

In the Bible, a cloud is not just something to do with the weather. When Israel walked out of Egypt, 'the Lord went before them by day in a pillar of cloud' (Exodus 13.21f.). The cloud was a sign that God went with them. In it, God's glory appeared. When Moses scaled Sinai to stand before the Lord, the Lord descended in a cloud (Exodus 34.5). It was likewise in a cloud that, later, he filled the tent of meeting with his presence (Exodus 40.34). In Numbers, the fourth Book of Moses, the cloud has become an established symbol of God's nearness. This connection is ratified in the historical books. What happens when the temple in Jerusalem is finished, the building work all done? What makes a mere massive building into a sanctuary? At the moment of dedication, 'a cloud filled the house of the Lord, so that the ministers could not stand to minister because of the cloud; for the glory of the Lord filled the house' (2 Chronicles 5.13f.). The cloud is glory. The glory is presence. It tells us that the Lord, the Father of all, is *there*.

If we read the Ascension story in this context, it no longer leaves us perplexed. On the contrary, the conclusion of Christ's earthly ministry is found to be continuous with a long history of God's self-revelation. In terms of Christ's own career, the Ascension cloud recalls the cloud that covered the Mount of Transfiguration, from which, Luke tells us, the Father's voice announced, 'This is my beloved Son' (9.35). It also points forward to the Lord's definitive coming at the end of time. Again, Luke gives us the very words of Jesus. Speaking of tribulations to come, he assures the disciples that they will see 'the Son of Man coming in a cloud with power and great glory' (21.27). The cloud will announce that the fullness of time is at hand.

Do you see? On Ascension Day, Christ does not disappear beyond earth's orbit. He enters the glory of the Father whereof the earth is full. He effectively fulfils his promise not to leave us orphans. To apprehend this new mode of Jesus' presence among us, special grace is called for. We need the Consoler, the Caller-to-mind, who will be our source of strength. Christ promises to send him 'soon'. Throughout Eastertide we have verified that what he says is sure. This word, too, will be fulfilled. Like the apostles, then, let us savour Christ's Ascension 'full of joy', waiting with eager expectation for the Father's promise at Pentecost.

PENTECOST

Acts 2.1-11:
There appeared to them tongues of fire,
resting on each of them.

Galatians 5.16-25:
The desires of the Spirit are against the flesh.

John 15.26f.; 16.12-15:
All he tells you will be taken from what is mine.

Pentecost marks the culmination of Eastertide. Today
the trinitarian mystery of God is finally revealed: God
bestows himself on us in fullness. Today the Church, born
on Calvary, is confirmed in its mission. Today we believers
receive power to confess Jesus' name with boldness. From
today it is given us to know God's indwelling. God would
make of each of us a tabernacle carrying his presence into
the world. Pentecost enables our personal engagements
as Christians. Yet the Spirit remains a mystery. Father
and Son suggest familiar categories. But how can we
conceive of the Spirit? It took the Church four hundred
years to express its doctrine of the Spirit's procession
from the Father through the Son. All the while, of course,
the Spirit *worked*. But remained beyond ready definition.
The Spirit's fruits are love, joy, peace, patience, kindness,
goodness, trustfulness, gentleness and self-control
(Galatians 5.22f.). These are strong virtues; stronger than
any violence. But at the same time, unprepossessing. The
Spirit is at once tranquillity and force. In himself he stays
a secret, yet he shows himself by what he does, in works
of transformation. To know him better, we might reflect
on his manifestation that morning in Jerusalem.

The coming of the Spirit spoken of in Acts is alarming.
A rush of wind announces flames descending from on

high. Both wind and fire are familiar from Old Testament epiphanies. The Lord is known to ride 'on the wings of the wind' (Psalm 103.3). While the wind did not show him to Elijah, it told the prophet he was coming (1 Kings 19.11ff.). The fire makes us think of Sinai's bush and of the pillar that guided Israel's exodus from Egypt (Exodus 3.2; 13.21).

There is something reassuring about fire. The hearth is a symbol of domestic bliss. We love candlelight and cosy fireplaces. But fire can also be terrible. Once, as a child, I watched a neighbour's farm burn down. I was in the village hall for a function when fire broke out next door. In no time, familiar buildings turned into a blazing inferno. All was destroyed. I remember the boy whose home it was, how he looked on aghast. I hope I shall never again see anything like it.

We shouldn't domesticate the Spirit. It comforts, yes, but also devours. It is a refiner's fire. Anything in us that is not gold will perish like chaff. A certain literature of cheap spirituality would have us think that the Spirit's gifts are mere accoutrements; improving additions to our normal self; functions of interior design. Not so. To pray for the coming of the Spirit takes courage. It requires a will to be re-made, to be made new.

The presence of the Spirit is revealed round about when the apostles speak, each in a foreign language, 'as the Spirit gave them utterance'. This fact is interesting. The diversity of languages is linked in the Bible with divine chastisement. Before Babel, all people spoke one tongue. Man's presumption caused God to fragment speech, to avert humanity's self-destructive purpose. One might expect that, at Pentecost, the Spirit would make everyone speak once more a *single* language. The opposite happens. The apostles, Aramaic-speakers all, address pilgrims from every corner of the world, each in his own language. This teaches a lesson. The Spirit doesn't impose uniformity. It reconciles diversity. The Church is a living testimony to this fact. From earliest times it has been *catholic*, that is, 'all-embracing'. In the Church, there is space for all who truly wish to put on Christ Jesus. Every voice contributes to a single polyphony of praise. In the Church, threads of every colour are woven together in a single seamless garment, fascinating in its beauty. This catholicity wrought by the Spirit is demanding. Who among us doesn't wish, at times, that the people we live and worship with were a little more like us? Yet the Church resists attempts to reduce this range of colours to a nondescript beige. It is alert to the death we incur when trying to quench the Spirit, reducing him to our small measure.

'When the Advocate comes,' says Jesus, 'you will be my witnesses.' Those words are addressed to us. The Spirit is not given for private enjoyment. It is given to be shared. The colour for Pentecost is red. Red is also the colour for martyrs. Almost all the apostles, first partakers of the Spirit, met violent death for Christ's sake. The Spirit gave them fortitude and grace to remain faithful. Let us pray that we may be worthy heirs. Let us surrender all selfishness and sin to be burnt in the Spirit's flame, that love may be kindled! Let us gratefully join the polyglot chorus of catholic voices in a single confession: Jesus Christ, the vanquisher of death, is Lord. He is our hope, our salvation, our joy. The Spirit equips each of us to make that confession in a language all our own, with the unique accents of our particular history, life and personality. It is for us, now, to proclaim God's mighty works. There are people out there who depend on the word of life you and I have to transmit, through Christ, in the Spirit.

TRINITY SUNDAY

Deuteronomy 4.32-34, 39f.:
Was there ever a word so majestic?

Romans 8.14-17:
The Spirit makes us cry out, Abba, Father!

Matthew 28.16-20:
Know that I am with you always.

It is customary on Trinity Sunday for bishops to issue a pastoral letter to be read in place of the homily. It is said that this is because bishops fear their priests will lapse into heresy if left to preach themselves. Many priests, true, have a dread of today's feast, not because they do not believe that God is three-in-one, not because they do not love the trinitarian mystery, but because it is so hard to talk about it. This shouldn't surprise us. God is by definition greater than anything we can think up or imagine. It is his nature to be transcendent. He reveals himself to us for love, but our minds are inadequate to grasp what is revealed. St Augustine, one of the acutest minds the Church has known, wrote at the end of his treatise on the Trinity: 'Free me, Lord, from a multitude of words!'[90] Having written that immortal book, he looked back over it and thought: it would be better to say nothing than to speak so inadequately. We know how he felt. Yet we crave illumination. We wish to comprehend. We have to say *something*. This year, the See of Nottingham being vacant, there is no pastoral letter to hide behind. So let us apply our minds in humility, proceeding by the surest route, that is, distilling the message given by the Church through the Scriptures.

In our reading from Deuteronomy, Moses asks: 'Was there ever a word so majestic?' What word is he talking about? No statement as such, but a 'word' in the sense we hear it spoken of in Luke's account of Christ's birth, when the shepherds say, 'Let us go to Bethlehem and see *this word* which the Lord has made known to us' (2.15). The 'word' is an event, a revelation, a communal experience. The 'word' Moses has in mind is a crucial one. Paraphrasing, we hear him say to the Israelites: 'We know that the God we confess is Lord of all. We know he created heaven and earth. We can sort of understand that. We can deal with the idea of an ultimate principle, a power beyond all power. If you see this, you see truth. But not the whole truth. There is more to it. This great, exalted, all-powerful God has stretched out his hand to save us. He has touched our lives. He has claimed us for himself. He has given tangible proof that he cares for us; has plans for us; entrusts us with a mission; wishes us to flourish. Was there ever a word so majestic?' This is what Moses says. It is the first lesson by which we come to know our trinitarian God. He is a God not enclosed in himself. He reaches out. He is present, merciful. St John would say: he is love. To love is to be vulnerable. We know that from experience. That, too, tells us much about God, one-in-three. He is omnipotent, but not frightening.

St Paul takes this insight further. Not only, he tells us, does God reach out and touch our lives. He is not just a kindly puppeteer. With the gift of Christ and the coming of the Spirit, God has drawn infinitely closer. He has drawn us into the mystery of himself, of his inner life of love in relation. By grace, that life, the life of God, pulsates in our created being. It is made manifest in deep longing. We recognize that longing by an impulse in our hearts that cries, 'Abba! Father!' Moses' 'majestic word' becomes a lived reality for each of us: we know we stand in a necessary, life-giving relationship with God; we know that without that relation we are incomplete. We rediscover ourselves as children, longing for our Father's love. Our God is a God who delights in sharing himself. He pours himself out, gives himself freely, and receives with open arms the love we show him in return. The Trinity is movement; movement and gift; gift and grace. It is freedom. It is joy.

Jesus' parting words to his disciples are a commission to spread this communion of divine life as widely as possible: 'Go, make disciples of all nations; baptize them in the name of the Father and of the Son and of the Holy Spirit, and teach them to observe all the commands I gave you.' If we have some inkling of God's love, we will be drawn to draw others into it. If we feel jealous of our faith; if we hoard graces received; if we want to keep others out of our private sanctuary: well, then we do not know God, Father, Son and Spirit. Then we are worshipping an idol. Our triune God shares himself infinitely while remaining undiminished. That is the mystery of the Trinity. The desire of God, Father, Son and Spirit, is to attract all mankind into their current of divine love, which is the source of all life, the foundation of all things, visible and invisible.

We give thanks to God for this gift of his life, bestowed on us in the Church. We give thanks to him for our communion with each other, for the friendship and love that give us some sense of who God is. We wish to put our lives at the disposal of his kingdom, as ministers of his outpoured grace. We wish to keep true to his word. And so we make a fresh resolve to adore our adorable God in spirit and in truth, standing silently before him in wonder, awe and praise.

5

ORDINARY TIME

2. SUNDAY, YEAR C

Isaiah 62.1-5:
As the bridegroom rejoices in his bride,
so will your God rejoice in you.

1 Corinthians 12.4-11:
There are varieties of gifts, but the same Spirit.

John 2.1-11:
There was a wedding at Cana in Galilee.

To make public statements about marriage is potentially incendiary these days, even in the backwater calm of a rural abbey church. Future cultural historians looking back on the shifting perceptions of marriage over the past half-century will express astonishment. In a dizzyingly short time we have moved from a mind-set that considered divorce an unspeakable transgression and still spoke of 'illegitimate children' to one that regards a position upholding marriage as a binding contract between one man and one woman as outrageously conservative. This is neither the time nor the place to analyse the reasons behind such change. It matters, however, that, as Catholics, we are conscious of how out of synch we are with the views of society at large. To be out of synch is not necessarily to be wrong. In his Rule, St Benedict warns against ceding too easily to majority opinion. It may transpire, he insists, that the minority is in fact the *sanior pars*, that is, of sounder judgement.

Not that there is consensus within the Church on this matter. The debate that followed Pope Francis's *Amoris laetitia* manifested divided sensibilities. The debate hinged on the thorny question of whether Catholics divorced and remarried can be admitted to Communion. If you will forgive me for stating my frank opinion: I consider this subject a red herring. Not that I wish to trivialize it. We all know of marriages that have broken down. We know the pain that can ensue. We know there isn't unfailingly someone at *fault*. It can happen that spouses grow apart or come to the realization they entered their sacramental union without knowing themselves or the other well enough. That such situations arise pertains to the woundedness of our world. The Church knows a lot about such wounds. It has remedies for them. Not for nothing does the Holy Father like to liken the Church to a field hospital. It would be perverse, though, to see nothing but wounds and so, gradually, to forget what a healthy body looks like. It would be wrong to define ourselves in terms of the crutches and casts we may need for longer or shorter times of convalescence.

Our readings invite us to consider marriage in its original, pristine aspect, as intended by our Creator. It is striking that they set out, not from the infatuation of Harry and Sally, but from an account of God's eternal love for mankind. Our passage from Isaiah insists that *the land* shall be called 'Married'; that *the Lord* will rejoice over Israel 'as the bridegroom rejoices over his bride'. This isn't just devotional embroidery. It's a statement of vital truth. It tells us this: if, as fragile human beings, we are at all capable of definitive self-giving, it is because God, who made us and keeps us in being, gives himself to us. Our fidelity is but a reflection of his. It presupposes the stability and grace only he can provide. To give myself irrevocably, from an undivided heart, to another is to enter into the mystery of love by which the world exists. It is a consecration of self that has cosmic dimensions.

This is no less true for the monk than for married men and women, for the monk's profession, too, has a nuptial character. It, too, enacts a covenanted bond that confirms the immemorial truth: 'it is not good for man to be alone'; it stands for the realization that only by entrusting myself to another (and receiving the other in trust) do I truly become who I am. The individual I count as longs to be recognized, then known, and finally loved as a *person*. When this happens, I am changed; my heart is enlarged; a capacity for love is released that, were I to stay locked in myself, would atrophy or implode. 'You shall be a crown of beauty', says the Lord; 'You shall no longer be termed Forsaken'; 'You shall be called, My Delight is in Her'. Who among us does not long for assurance of this kind? Who would not long to live up to it?

That the incarnate Son of God should first reveal his glory at a wedding says a lot. Christ came to render effective the promise Isaiah foretold. God became man to restore our nature from within, to fill the empty, dust-grimed vessels of our lives, vessels repeatedly chipped and bruised, with new wine, to prepare us for a spousal intimacy of love with himself so that – even here, now – we might live that love on in transformative commitments. Whatever disappointments and hurts we may have known, this is our calling. This is the core of the Christian condition. We have but to invite the Lord in for this mystery to start unfolding, as long as we heed Mary's words: 'Do *whatever* he tells you.' Even as marriage is based on the freedom of the spouses, the Lord does not force himself on us. He beckons, instructs, promises. But it is for us to give the gift of our integral assent. This Eucharist is for us an occasion to utter that Yes in gratitude and joy.

8. SUNDAY, YEAR A

Isaiah 49.14-15:
Does a woman forget her baby at the breast?

2 Corinthians 4.1-5:
People must think of us as Christ's servants.

Matthew 6.24-34:
No one can be the slave of two masters.

Slavery is a difficult notion. It may trouble us that Scripture speaks of it a lot. I say, 'a lot', though this has not always been apparent. Biblical language has been buffed up to cover difficult subjects with gloss. If you look up 'slave' in the Authorized Version, you will find only two occurrences in the entire Bible, the relevant semantic field being covered by the less offensive word 'servant'. A modern version like the New English Translation has no such scruples. It uses the word 'slave' 250 times. There can be no doubt: this latter option is closer to the original texts. In the Old Testament, slavery is above all connected with Israel's two exiles, first in Egypt, then in Babylon. Remember: God foretold their lot of slavery right from the outset of his call. In chapter 15 of Genesis, the passage in which God shows Abram the night sky thick with stars and says, 'So shall your descendants be', he also says, 'know for certain that your descendants will sojourn in a land not theirs, and will be slaves there.' The experience of servitude is crucial to Israel's self-understanding. It recalls the reality of salvation. It matters to be mindful of that from which God set them free. The Pentateuch enjoins repeatedly, 'Remember that you were slaves in Egypt.'

Such historical remembrance is all very well. The greater the distance in time, the less humiliating memories become. The trouble is, Scripture posits enslavement no less as a present reality. Jesus proclaims that he has come to liberate his people. From what? The insinuation of *un*freedom caused some hearers to boil with rage: 'We are sons of Abraham and have never been anyone's slaves!' (John 8.33). How deluded we can get in our efforts to keep up appearances. That is why the work of grace has the habit of making our facades collapse, of pulling down our masks. How else can the God of truth engage with us? It means nothing to confess Christ as my Saviour, come to set me free, if I do not recognize myself as somehow captive. This is the foundation of my Christian life. I need to stand firm upon it.

Recently, on a train journey, I listened to a podcast of *Desert Island Discs* from 1999. The castaway was Clarissa Dickson Wright, one of that redoubtable duo of TV cooks, the Two Fat Ladies, a woman of uncommon accomplishments: in her day a celebrated lawyer; later a culinary historian; known to have knocked out an Alsatian with her bare fists. She was also a publicly recovering alcoholic. She describes what became for her a turning point, at the height (or in the depth) of addiction. One day, while she was making jam, her pot boiled over. She had to kneel down to remove the sticky stuff from the kitchen floor. 'I hadn't prayed for years', she says, 'and was too arrogant to ask for help, but because I was on my knees I said, "Dear God, if you're up there, I really can't go on."' This was, she insists a 'cry from the heart'. It was answered forthwith, robustly. The following day she was arrested for drunk driving. She was brought face to face with facts, seeing herself as she was, from the outside, as it were. She sought help and got it. The Demon Drink would never again usurp her life. Having owned her enslavement, she could be set free.[91]

There was no mystic rapture in the kitchen. The scene, on the face of it, is trivial, sad, swimming in an alcoholic daze. And yet it reveals itself, in fact, as a moment of grace. The jam-spattered tiles became a Damascus road. Clarissa's Ananias was a bobby on booze patrol. How important it is (but how hard) to recognize our humiliations, the times we dread, the stuff of nightmares, as potential epiphanies. They are just that, in so far as they help us establish a new base in truth and let go of illusions that stand in the way, not only of our flourishing, but of our life with God. Certain forms of unfreedom are more obvious than others. Lives are blighted by addictions to drink, drugs, sex or other compulsive behaviours. Our Gospel reminds us, though, that subtle forms of slavery entrap us even if we may be spared the more explicit kinds. We are challenged to examine where our treasure is and ask: '*Am* I free – or not? Am I bound by possessions, status or comfort, by fear or by some old resentment?' In the words of today's Collect, God would settle us 'untroubled' under his 'peaceful rule' – the only kind of dominion that is perfect freedom. But for that to happen we must surrender the password to our prison. It may seem more than we can face. We may feel overwhelmed by weariness or shame. We may be apprehensive. In prison, at least we know where we are; a lily of the field meanwhile stands fearfully exposed. We may think wistfully that in any case 'the Lord has forgotten me'. Isaiah lets us hear the Lord's response: 'Does a woman forget her sucking child, that she should have no compassion for the child of her womb?' Let us entrust ourselves to God's freeing possession. Let us run the risk of freedom. And let us, for goodness' sake, stop pretending.

14. SUNDAY, YEAR B

Ezekiel 2.2-5:
I send you to the people of Israel, to a nation of rebels.

2 Corinthians 12.7-10:
A thorn was given me in the flesh.

Mark 6.1-6:
This is the carpenter, surely?

At an important turning point in Evelyn Waugh's novel, *Brideshead Revisited*, Sebastian, back from Sunday Mass, says to Charles: 'Oh dear, it's very difficult being a Catholic.'[92] Charles is baffled: he has never found religion impinging much on the life of his friend, except as a formal observance of atavistic ritual. Sebastian's admission is a signpost to an inner life of struggle of which Charles had been quite unaware. It marks the beginning of an estrangement set to create a growing distance between the two friends.

We may all find faith 'hard' at times. We may moan casually about it. What is it, though, that is so difficult? Mostly, I dare say, it is not Catholic *practice*, but rather faith as such, the task of remaining open to, of consciously engaging in, a reality that is transcendent. Much militates against such engagement. Contrary to what we may assume, this has always been the case: it's hardly harder to believe today than it was in ages past. Scripture is forthright in naming the impulses that can give rise to practical atheism, an attitude that would make us think God does not exist or, at any rate, that he has no interest in us, so can lay no claim to obedience or homage. Our readings offer three different perspectives on obstacles to religious belief.

Our first reading is from Ezekiel. The passage follows hard on the heels of the book's majestic introduction, one of the Bible's most explicit accounts of theophany: of mortal humanity standing face to face with the uncreated Godhead. Ezekiel acquires existential knowledge of just how inadequate he is to know eternal realities. His consciousness of God's exaltedness and man's lowliness saturates every statement he makes. This otherness of God also accounts, at least in part, for the unbelief of the people to whom he must prophesy. 'Till now', the Lord tells him, 'the Israelites and their ancestors have been in revolt against me.' Revolts are plentiful in the history of Israel. They are caused, almost invariably, by the people's sense that the Lord is too far away. 'Is the Lord among us, or not?' The question occurs at regular intervals during the exodus. Often, Israel acts as if the Lord was not, and makes alternative provision, as in the moulding of the golden calf. Do not we, too, at times prefer gods of our making?

While the prophet speaks of unbelief sprung from God's awesomeness, the Gospel presents disdain born of familiarity. 'This is the carpenter, surely, the son of Mary?' The fact of having lived alongside the Lord inoculates the people of Nazareth against believing him to be anything special. It can be difficult to accept a word of truth from someone close to us. We can be blind to the virtues, even the sanctity, of those among whom we live. This attitude threatens to affect our spiritual life, too. We take the Lord's gifts for granted, forgetting the standards they presuppose. We skip confession on the grounds that we've done nothing out of the ordinary. We lose the sense of what happens at Mass, or become deaf to the presence of the Lord in his Word. And so, gradually, we fall away, surrendering to un-faith and indifference.

St Paul alerts us to a more interior drama. What in his case impeded faith was a 'thorn in the flesh'. It seemed to him a contradiction of God's goodness. Everything, he was sure, would be better without it. He would be a better servant of the Gospel. He prayed: 'Lord, take it away!' His prayer went unheeded. This fact provoked a crisis of faith. What was Paul's 'thorn'? Who knows. We can consult our own experience, the sorts of things that make you and me feel disadvantaged in the things of God: illness or chronic pain, perhaps, or some psychological wound; a mistake we have made that has left traces on our heart or body; a temperamental deficiency. The possibilities are many. But who among us has never thought, in the secret of our heart, 'If only God would free me from this, I would believe; I would be a fervent Christian, a person fully alive.' Perhaps we are wrong. Perhaps the 'thorn' has a purpose for us as it did for Paul. Perhaps it is meant to keep us from thinking too highly of ourselves, from supposing too much on our own strength.

The remedy for all three forms of unbelief is the same: an act of deliberate faith in the providence of God. There may not be much sweet sentiment in such an act. That is neither here nor there. What matters is to receive from God's hand whatever he gives, be it high or lowly; to strive to perceive the mystery with which this world is charged, to see this mystery as real, to remain at its level. In a moment I will invite you to 'lift up your hearts'. That is the key posture for anyone seeking faith. Lift up your heart always, let it tend towards the Lord, and he will come to you, at once sublime and unconscionably near, revealing even your wounds to be signs of his predilection.

14. SUNDAY, YEAR C

Isaiah 66.10-14:
Towards her I send flowing peace, like a river.

Galatians 6.14-18:
The world is crucified to me, and I to the world.

Luke 10.1-12, 17-20:
Let your first words be, 'Peace to this house!'

Our readings today all speak of peace. They do so in different registers, in different tones of voice; but the fundamental theme is the same. In Isaiah the Lord promises that peace will come to Jerusalem 'flowing like a river' – an evocative image in a context of regular drought. In the Gospel we hear how the 72 were sent out in pairs to proclaim the Good News, instructed to begin always with the greeting, 'Peace to this house.' In the Epistle, Paul, tired of worry for the churches, asks to be left in peace. 'I want no more trouble from anyone after this,' says he, revealing the frustration that cannot but be part of ecclesiastical governance, today as in the first century. And what about you and me? Do we long for peace? Are we bearers and givers of peace? Or do we simply want others to stop interfering with our own, privatized sense of peace? There is plenty of scope, here, for self-examination.

For a Christian, peace is both an ethical imperative and a promise of beatitude. We have inherited this dual focus from Judaism. We are placed in this world to tend it, form it, enhance it, share its fruits and know its sweetness; but the prosperity we may know here below is a pointer towards a greater, spiritual reality. It is the harmony reigning between the transcendent goal and the present reality that constitutes peace. This principle of universal application is embedded in the preaching of Isaiah. His crowning vision of peace cascading like a river is from the book's final chapter. Having painted a canvas of epic proportions, having spoken of promise and betrayal, of grace and sin, of vocation and rejection, of exile and homecoming, Isaiah's prophecy concludes by pointing towards an ecstasy of peace. It is not about individuals feeling peaceful. It is about a people that, at long last, after many trials, has learnt to carry out God's will and to realize God's purpose. To know God's peace, we must be disposed to harbour peace. To harbour peace, we must live on its terms. To live on the terms of peace we have to conform our wills, our lives, to God's commandments, then be willing to invite others into the peace that ensues. Let us bear this aspect of obligation in mind when, later in this Mass, we offer each other with quiet reverence a sign of peace.

The exasperated tone in our passage from Galatians, with the apostle saying, 'Oh, leave me in peace!' is occasioned by the church's failure to see what it means to know real peace. With the incarnation of the Son of God, peace assumed personal features. In another letter Paul says, in words of signal importance, that it is Christ who *is* our peace (Ephesians 2.14). Christ is peace, not chiefly because of what he taught, but because of what he did for us. We are sometimes apt to be confused about the distinction. We speak of 'the Gospel' as if it were a manual of decent living, as if the pursuit of earthly justice and peace were the hallmark of the Christian. Decent living, justice and concord matter, by all means. They set a seal of authenticity on the Christian life. But the peace Christ bestows is more essential. It springs from his sacrifice, offered on the cross to the Father, by which sin is pardoned, death conquered and the grace of transformation offered freely. For a Christian, peace is not first and foremost political. 'Peace and mercy', Paul tells us, are outward effects of the inward process by which we are made into 'an altogether new creature'.

The peace we, like the 72 disciples in the Gospel, are charged to carry far and wide is a sign and pledge of this newness. It is not our possession but God's free gift. As always with God's gifts, the more freely we share it, the greater does our share in it become. The Gospel always sees this visible world in connection with the kingdom of God mysteriously forming in our midst. The kingdom is the Church, Christ's mystical body, at once visible in those who bear the sign of Christ and invisible in those who, without being marked with the sign, nonetheless have a share in grace and a longing for redemption. The kingdom will only be fully revealed after the resurrection of the flesh. The world we know now, even at its most luminous, cannot, must not, be confused with God's kingdom; but we are called, within this world, to hasten the kingdom's coming, to make all things ready. The Christian's peace, the peace Christ bestows, is peace 'not of this world'. It presupposes free detachment. We are to cherish the world, to work faithfully within it. At the same time, we are to long more and more for the partial to pass and for what is whole and lasting to appear. The Christian condition is defined by this tension, which is sometimes piercingly painful. Still, however paradoxical it sounds: to accept this tension, to surrender to it, even to learn to love it, is to know Christ's peace, which passes all understanding.

17. SUNDAY, YEAR A

1 Kings 3.5,7-12:
Give me a heart to understand how to discern between good and evil.

Romans 8.28-30:
God works for good with those who love him.

Matthew 13.44-52:
The kingdom of heaven is like a dragnet cast into the sea.

Over several months we have, from different countries and continents, heard newly enthroned rulers proclaim proud manifestos. None has been an anointed king, though of one it has been said that he fancies himself to be a cross between Jesus, Jupiter and Louis XIV.[93] That indicates more than an average degree of self-confidence. In such a climate, there is something refreshing about the sentiment voiced by Solomon. Risen to the Davidic throne, he saw God in a dream. Asked what he would have God give him, Solomon replied: 'I am but a little child; I do not know how to go out or come in.' God's people, he said, is so great; I, so inconsequential! Might the Lord, then, grant this: 'an understanding mind to govern thy people, that I may discern between good and evil'. A leader who is humble and has esteem for the people he rules! A head of state with a sense of right and wrong! Who wouldn't wish to be led by one such? It pleased God that Solomon asked as he did. Assurance was given that his prayer would be granted. Here, we might think, is Solomon's career in a nutshell, a function of noble aspiration and divine favour. This would, however, be a superficial reading – almost a travesty – of the Hebrew Bible's subtle account.

We need only look to the previous chapter of 1 Kings, the introduction, as it were, to Solomon's prayer. Here, we read how Solomon inaugurated his rule, displaying violent determination. First, he ordered the execution of his elder brother Adonijah, a pretender to the throne. Next, he sent Abiathar the priest into exile. Joab, the commander of the army, was killed at Solomon's command even as he clung to the horns of the altar, an asylum supposed to be inviolable. Finally, Shimei, a vocal descendant of the house of Saul, was put to death by royal decree. In one fell swoop, Solomon eliminated competition from within his family, from the priestly caste, from the military, and from his one dynastic rival. Having got this business out of the way, he went off and married the daughter of Pharaoh, thus striking an alliance with the nation that embodies idolatry and faithlessness in the Old Testament.

This is the Solomon who protested to the Lord, 'I am but a little child' – a disingenuous confession, surely? Well, yes and no. On the one hand Solomon was a ruthless prince, set to eliminate any obstacle threatening his career; on the other hand, he sought divine wisdom and displayed great sagacity. He was entrusted with the building of the temple, the tabernacle in which God would be present to his people. His prayer of dedication is among the Bible's most exalted passages. Yet he was at the same time a scoundrel and a philanderer of the first order. Easily seduced by carnal passion, Solomon 'loved many foreign women'. This generic statement is itemized: he had '700 wives, and 300 concubines, and his wives turned away his heart' (1 Kings 11.3). Solomon, the wise, was no less the fool who went after Chamos, Molech and other foreign gods. He did 'what was evil in the sight of the Lord and did not wholly follow the Lord' (1 Kings 11.6). He incurred God's wrath. Through Solomon's sin, Israel lost its integrity. The division of Israel and Judah was punishment for Solomon's iniquity. The man who completed the construction of the kingdom also pulled it apart.

There is a lesson, and it is this: that few are the people on this earth who are wholly good or wholly bad; that someone whose morals are deplorable may yet be wisdom's mouthpiece; that one entrusted with high office may be subject to titanic inner struggles, which, at vulnerable times, may cause him or her to slip terribly; that the confluence of good and bad conditions the lives of all of us; and that this shouldn't come as a surprise. Solomon asked for a mind to discern between evil and good. The answer wasn't given on a postcard, but in the form of a battle with self that would perdure until he drew his last breath. In today's Gospel, the Lord likens the kingdom to a dragnet full of fish, some good, some bad. It's an image that applies to the Church, yes, of course, but no less to the human heart; for remember, 'the kingdom of God is within you' (Luke 17.21). We easily take it for granted that we are good whereas the bad is in others. The example of Solomon teaches us that, no, it is not so.

If we dare to make his prayer our own, let's be ready to find all sorts of fish in the deep waters of our own heart, and let's sort them wisely and courageously. If we heed this call, we might acquire genuine humility. We might, too, be graced with compassion as we come to see that our neighbour's battle is every bit as hard as ours; that, when our brother falls, we shouldn't sneer, but should offer him a hand to help him rise and resume his ascent towards the good. For that is where our deepest longing is bound, even when a lower instinct would drag us down the other way. God grant us grace to know which is which.

30. SUNDAY, YEAR A

Exodus 22.20-26:
You must not molest the stranger or oppress him.

1 Thessalonians 1.5-10:
You were led to become imitators of the Lord.

Matthew 22.34-40:
On these commandments hangs the whole Law, and the Prophets also.

May I ask you to look up for a moment, towards the space above your heads, towards the ceiling? Our church, for being neo-Gothic and helped, in construction, by techniques unavailable to our medieval forebears, still reveals the soaring majesty of the style: its vast airiness, its suggestion of stone in flight. This effect is made possible by a discovery that revolutionized architecture and, with it, the Western imagination. Briefly told, eleventh-century master builders worked out new ways in which to make designated parts of a building bear the weight of the whole. By carefully calculated buttresses and arches, they made their churches rise to unmatched elegance and height. Immense Gothic edifices rose upon simple skeletons of structural features. If you compromise the structure, the building falls, its apparent self-evidence reduced to a heap of prettily carved rubble.

It is good to bear this image in mind as we reflect on Our Lord's words regarding the two great commandments of love: on them, he says, 'hangs the whole Law, and the Prophets also'. On them hangs our credibility as Christians. If we fail to obey these commandments, no amount of strict observance will suffice to point our lives heavenward. However hard we slog in the quarry of rigour, without charity's lofty, carrying arch, the stones we produce will not stay one on top of the other.

This places us before a major problem: what if we have no love, or only very little? What if our heart seems shrivelled up, unyielding of any sweet feeling either towards the Lord or towards our neighbour? Are we then counted reprobate? Given how much depends on our love, these questions are urgent, and deserve an answer. The first thing to say is this: we must not reduce love to a matter of sentiment. We're apt to do that, these days, often led to believe that the deepest truth about ourselves is what we feel like. It is curious that we should fall for this illusion when every day offers ample occasion to ascertain how inconstant, how fickle our feelings are. What is more, feelings come, feelings go. They are largely beyond our rational control. No one, not even Almighty God, can command us to feel this or that. Let us be reassured by this. The true nature of love must be found elsewhere.

When Christ enjoins the two commandments of love, he says nothing new. He cites the Mosaic code. With good reason, the liturgy gives us a passage from this code as our first reading, to show what it means to love in practice. First, we are told, 'do not molest the stranger or oppress him': be generous and hospitable, open your heart to the misfortune of others, mindful that you were a stranger once, and may be so again. Second, 'be not harsh with the widow or orphan': do not ride roughshod over those whose position in society is weak. Third, 'do not play the usurer': do not grow rich from the necessity of others. And fourth, 'if you take another's coat as pledge, you must give it back to him before sunset'.

This precept never fails to move me. It shows us much about who God is, about how we must act to imitate him. It tells us: don't merely stand on your rights. Such an attitude is arrogant and tedious. Let your principles be tempered by humanity. What if that cloak is all the other fellow has to cover him at night, and the night is cold? Train yourself to look on life from perspectives other than your own. What happens then is wonderful. Your heart grows vulnerable, which is painful; but it also becomes sensitive to deep, essential things, which is glorious. The heart emerges from the icebox of self-sufficiency. 'I am full of pity,' says the Lord (Exodus 22.27). We are to be, too, and to act accordingly. That is what it is to love. In our Collect, we have prayed, 'Make us love what you command'. We learn to love by doing. This week, in the refectory, our community heard the following story read:

> One day, a man who was visiting Mount Athos asked several wise elders the following question: 'What is the most important thing in your life?' Each time he was answered like this: 'It is divine love; to love God and to love one's neighbour.' He said: 'I don't have love, either for prayer, or for God, or for other people. What must I do?' And then he decided by himself: 'I will act as if I had love.' Thirty years later, the Holy Spirit gave him the grace of love.[94]

There is a lesson here for all of us – and, while 30 years is a long time, the lesson is full of encouragement. It tells us that God entrusts us with a task, and gives us grace to accomplish it no matter what we feel like. To become a Christian is to live differently, to learn a new language of being. Acquiring fluency takes time. But what a noble mission: to draw divine pity down on earth that it may, in time, bear fruit, in love, within us and around us. Why not muster the courage to ask: 'What is the most important thing in my life?' Then to be prepared to review our choices, to renew our Christian purpose.

6

Saints

AN EASTER PILGRIMAGE TO BEAUVALE CHARTERHOUSE

For years, I lived in a house in which hung a reproduction of Zurbarán's portrait of St John Houghton. I loved it from the first time I saw it. Zurbarán was arguably the greatest painter of the Spanish golden age. He produced his picture for the Charterhouse of Jerez a century after Fr Houghton's death. By then, the Carthusian was revered across Europe as a martyr. It is not a dramatic painting, however. There's no blood, no gore, no cruel crowd. Houghton stands alone in his snow-white habit, looking intently ahead, his eyes fixed on something, somebody. Zurbarán excelled elsewhere in depicting mystic ecstasy. If you look out his *St Francis in Meditation* in the National Gallery, you'll see what I mean. There is nothing ecstatic about Houghton, though. He is recollected, alert. He carries two emblems of his death. There is a noose around his neck; his right hand holds a stylized image of his heart. Why the heart? Having been drawn on a hurdle from the Tower of London to Tyburn, Houghton was hanged. He was then cut down before he was allowed to die, remaining conscious when his abdomen was opened with a knife and his entrails extracted. The executioner next put a hand on his heart, to wrench it out. At this Houghton exclaimed, 'Good Jesu! What will ye do with my heart?' These words are from a trustworthy account, recorded by a young man who stood close by. The noose and heart are symbolic codes referring to historical facts, historical outrage. Yet the painting breathes peace. There is a sweet, moving benevolence in Houghton's face; an expression of expectancy that could, one feels, erupt into a smile. It brings to mind the testimony of St Thomas More, who knew the London Carthusians well, having lived among them for four years in his youth. From his cell, he saw Fr Houghton, Fr Lawrence, the prior of Beauvale, and a third monk being led to Tower Gate. More cried out to his daughter, 'Dost thou not see, Meg, these blessed Fathers cheerfully going to their death as bridegrooms to their marriage?' The Spanish artist has captured this disposition. He has succeeded in making it credible. The concreteness of martyrdom is squarely put before us. But Houghton, with eyes wide open, sees through it and beyond it, infusing all the objective awfulness with joy. What does it take to forge a soul of such lucidity, such confidence?

The answer, I think, lies right before us, in the ruins of Beauvale. Houghton lived in this place for only a short time, some six months during 1531. But his daily round here would have been indistinguishable from the one he observed through long, faithful years in his principal home, the London Charterhouse, a few minutes' walk from the Barbican. As a young man he was driven by a yearning for the absolute. He had excellent worldly prospects, but they left him unengaged. 'He desired', said a contemporary who knew him well, 'like a morning stag to ascend the heights.' The image, thick with biblical allusions, is striking. Thirsting for the source of living water, yearning to breathe mountain air, John Houghton set out from homely thickets of restricted view. He started climbing. The setting for this alpine quest was his monk's cell. Monastic life is often thought of as a life of quiet retreat, an uneventful existence wafting on clouds of incense. There isn't a great deal of truth in such notions. From ancient times, monks have spoken of their life as a combat. The monastery is a battlefield in which competing forces in my heart brandish their arms. In solitude I am led to confront all I carry within me that is *not* good, *not* pure, *not* noble. I am invited to cast all this into the furnace of God's love, that my life, by grace, may be reformed. To persevere requires stamina. Not for nothing have monks likened their observance to a desert pilgrimage, to the scaling of a steep mountain.

John Houghton was given to this arduous progress. Through it, his natural gifts were refined, his conscience sharpened. His sense of what is good and true became compelling. The fortitude he showed at Tyburn was not simply innate. Integrity is something each of us must conquer. 'I have no love', says a Psalm, 'for half-hearted men' (118.113). To be whole-hearted women and men, we must let God's cleansing, re-creating work take place in our lives every day. We must be valiant, love truth, and keep the Lord before our eyes constantly. Today's Gospel speaks of the coming of the Spirit of Truth. It is sent, not just to adorn us like an ornament. It is a Spirit of commission. We are called to be witnesses to truth in a world that is increasingly seduced by falsehood. 'Always be prepared to make a defence to anyone who calls you to account for the hope that is in you' (1 Peter 3.15).

The example of our Carthusian saints shows at what cost such a defence may have to be made. Who knows what account you and I will be called upon to give in our times, our so strange times? Beauvale remains for us all, whatever our state of life, an image of spiritual conquest. The grace that has made this place holy has power to sanctify our lives, too, to make us whole, credible Christians, consecrated in the truth, with the courage to suffer, even to die, rather than to speak or act on a word we know to be untrue.[95]

10. The copy of Zurbarán's portrait of St John Houghton, a Cambridge alumnus, that hangs in Fisher House, the University's Catholic Chaplaincy.

22 APRIL: BLESSED MARIA GABRIELLA SAGHEDDU

Blessed Maria Gabriella, a nun of our Order, has left us a handful of letters. One of them I think of often. She received a vocation within a vocation during the octave of prayer for Christian Unity in 1936, when her abbess, the remarkable Mother Pia Gullini, invited the sisters to pray for an end to divisions among Christians. Sister Gabriella got permission to offer her life for this great cause. When a little later she developed tuberculosis, both she and Mother Pia took it for granted that her illness was linked to her pledge. The letter I have in mind was written the following year, shortly before she died. Entirely matter-of-factly, she said the following: 'I have made the Lord an offering of my life; he has shown me the honour of taking me at my word.'[96] She lets us touch a crucial truth of the Christian condition: its realism. She reminds us that what is given *is* given; that the pledges we give and receive are not a playing with words but real contracts. We take God's gifts for granted, perhaps, but do we let him do the same in our regard? We have all made gifts to the Lord. The main one was made for us at our baptism. This we have since confirmed: some by vows of matrimony; some by private pledges; some by monastic profession. By our own gift, our lives are not our own. What a difference it makes, then, at times when the Lord claims what we have given him, if, instead of sighing and groaning and feeling sorry for ourselves, we stand upright and dignified and say: 'I thank you Lord for showing me the honour of considering me a man or woman of my word!' That is how we grow towards the stature of Christ. That is how we find freedom, abundance of life, and joy.

23 APRIL: ST GEORGE

A few years ago, when the feast of St George was given the status of a liturgical solemnity in England, a spate of indignant letters appeared in the Catholic press. How, the refrain went, can bishops expect their sophisticated flock to honour a saint whose life is a naïve legend? Who believes in dragons anyway? Such moans show up a tendency endemic to our times: the tendency to think we are cleverer than people of ages past. But is the story of St George really so far beyond the pale?

References to the martyrdom of George are found from the fourth century onwards. There is general consensus about its main elements. George is said to have been a native of Cappadocia, in what we would think of as central Turkey. He is said to have given valiant witness to his faith during the reign of Diocletian; and to have paid for it with his life at Lydda in Palestine, just north of the present-day Gaza Strip. Pilgrims flocked to his shrine at Lydda in the sixth century, well before Gregory the Great sent Augustine to this island. That a soldier discovered to be a Christian should have incurred fierce punishment during the third-century Great Persecution is something we can take for granted; and it is far from unlikely that a Cappadocian should have found himself dispatched to the Eastern Mediterranean. People in late antiquity, especially when connected with the army, moved around a great deal more than we usually think. These, then, are the constitutive elements of the life of St George handed down to us. They are eminently credible and well attested.

The later *cult* of George, meanwhile, grew up around a more flourished account. We find it set down in the

Golden Legend of James of Voragine, a thirteenth-century Dominican, who wrote an anthology of saints' lives for the benefit of preachers. The book remained a bestseller for two centuries. Many Europeans will have known it, at least in part, by heart. We get an idea of what it meant for people if we recall that between 1470 and 1500, in the first generation of printing, at least 87 Latin editions of the *Legend* were produced, as well as 67 editions in various vernaculars. This is a lot more than all known printings of the Bible in any language during the same period.

It is James who describes how the young George helped some folks in a country town oppressed by a dragon, telling them: 'You have nothing to fear! Believe in Christ and be baptised, and I shall slay it.' They followed his counsel. He was true to his word. Four yoke of oxen were needed to cart away the carcass of the beast. George promptly gave the reward he had received to the destitute. James also provides details of George's trials in Palestine, telling us how a cruel official prepared for him a cauldron of molten lead, only to find George sitting down in it, after making the sign of the cross, 'as though he were in a refreshing bath'.[97]

Before we shout, 'Nonsense!', we might reflect on the kind of imagery we use to embellish bare bones of fact. Imagine a historian of the thirty-first century happening on a miraculously preserved book of Manga cartoons or an incorrupt DVD of a 2013 Hollywood 3D computer-generated extravaganza. Imagine him staring at the screen in disbelief and asking, 'Did they swallow *that*?' Consider how, to our way of thinking, he would have missed the point. Before we are rude about our forebears' primitive faith, we should refine our sense of their sense of imagery;

also of what they thought of as good entertainment. James of Voragine was a contemporary of Aquinas. He and Thomas entered the Order of Preachers the same year. His age was not inimical to stringent thinking. But it retained an ability to think in terms of symbols, an ability we, alas, have largely lost.

It was, however, the symbol of George, what he represented, that made him so well loved throughout the Middle Ages. Quite how he came to be patron saint of England we do not know, but he was honoured here long before the Norman Conquest. It is wonderful, I think, that we have as our patron a native of Cappadocia; in other words, a Turk. The choice shows what mattered to Englishmen of old when they constructed their identity: not ethnic criteria or narrow-minded jingoism rallying round a cricket team, but the generous living out of Christian faith through charity to the poor, help to those in need, and fearless confession in the face of secular might. These values are hardly less relevant today than they were in the third century. And I would say St George compares favourably to many a contemporary role model. If we put him alongside Justin Bieber or the Spice Girls, we may conclude that the medievals weren't so silly after all.

25 APRIL: ST MARK

A conceit sometimes used by Renaissance painters was that of painting themselves into their compositions, as participants in the scene they depicted. According to tradition, St Mark did a similar thing when writing his Gospel. Several ancient authors identify the evangelist with the young man we read of in chapter 14 of Mark's Gospel, who, when the soldiers who had arrested the

Lord grabbed his cloak to seize him, too, promptly slipped out of it and fled naked.

We cannot verify the identification, but on a symbolic level it is indisputably true. Eusebius of Caesarea, in the third century, tells us that Mark was the secretary of Peter and that his Gospel sets down the apostle's reminiscences.[98] Now, Peter's discipleship was marked by signal failures. It is striking to find these described with almost brutal precision by Mark: his Gospel portrays Peter sleeping soundly in Gethsemane, despite Jesus' plea, 'Stay awake!' (14.32-38); it shows him denying his Master not once or twice, but three times, 'with oaths', only to break down in bitter tears at his own weakness (14.66-72).

The first followers of Christ are not idealized by Mark but painted in true colours, colours with which we, you and I, can identify. And yet it is these very men of unsteady courage whom Jesus, after the Resurrection, sends out into the world to represent him: to work signs, to cast out demons, to tread on serpents, to heal the sick. And they *did* all those things! What is the lesson? That it is not natural courage that makes a faithful and true disciple, but the Lord's gift; readiness to let *his* strength work through *our* weakness, 'working with' us, in Mark's phrase (16.20). St Mark is said to have died a martyr's death in northern Egypt, faithful to the last. And so it is appropriate that this man, who once fled like a rabbit from the cross of Christ, is represented to us in the figure of a lion. There is hope for us all.

27 APRIL: ST RAFAEL ARNÁIZ BARÓN

A monk strives to heed Christ's command to lay down his life for his friends (John 15.13). There is no contradiction between this endeavour and a life of solitude. The contemplative life, for a Christian, is never merely an ascent of the alone towards the Alone. On the contrary, the more intimate our union with Christ, the more clearly we experience a living communion with all the members of his body; the more passionately we adhere to God's purpose, 'that all may be saved' (1 Timothy 2.4).

St Rafael made this intuition his own. In his diary he notes how, at the beginning of his monastic life, he used to feel let down by his brethren. He sought model monks, heroic ascetics, paragons of virtue. Instead he found very average people whose behaviour was not always consistent with their profession. 'How I suffered!' he says, before going on to stress that in this early outlook there had been 'plenty of pride, much vanity, and immense self-love'. As he progressed in the life of conversion and prayer, essential change occurred. Just listen:

> Now a very unusual thing is happening to me. Some days, when I come out from prayer, although it seems to me that I am doing nothing, I feel very strong desires, I yearn with a great longing to love all the members of the community as Jesus loves them. [...] Just as before I would become disturbed upon seeing a failure or a weakness in a brother and would almost feel revulsion, now I feel a very great tenderness towards him and would like to make reparation for the fault insofar as I can.[99]

This kind of change is the sole reliable proof that we really are making progress in our Christian life and prayer. Precisely because it goes against the grain of our human sensibility (and entirely exceeds human strength) it proves that Christ lives in us; that we are beginning to know the power of his love. Rafael speaks about the pain involved in the process. He also speaks of the immense freedom it brings. For it translates us into a new dimension of life, an infinitely broad and beautiful space where, in Anthony's phrase, Christ himself 'is the air we breathe'.[100]

17 JUNE: ST ALBAN

The drama of Alban's life and death, handed down to us by Bede in his *Ecclesiastical History*, was played out not far from here, in Hertfordshire, during the third century, when there were still people around who had known the successors to the apostles: St Alban seems to have overlapped with St Irenaeus, who had known St Polycarp, who had known St John the Evangelist. Today's feast reminds us that the roots of Christian witness in this land run deep.

Alban, we are told, sheltered a foreign priest fleeing persecution. Note, Alban was not a Christian at the time: he was simply a good man moved with pity for the plight of a fellow man in distress. Alban invited the priest into his house. So edified was he by the priest's devotion that he asked, after a while, to be baptized. When the pagan authorities discovered the priest's whereabouts, Alban surrendered himself instead of his guest, to be executed in substitution. He gave up his life for his friend – so great was his love. Alban the saint is revered for sheltering an alien whose faith, at first, was different from his own. This stranger became for him a brother. Their destinies became as one. The shrine of St Alban came to be a reference point for this nation, a sign of its people's highest aspirations.

Do we not need St Alban's example and prayers especially right now, when thoughtless, violent slogans cause blood to be shed to discredit the very ethos of hospitality, to keep strangers out? Many clamour to draw up the bridge and lower the portcullis. So we, you and I, should have the Christian charity and courage to keep Alban's legacy alive.[101]

21 JUNE: ST ALOYSIUS GONZAGA

St Aloysius, born Luigi Gonzaga in 1568, grew up grandly. His father was an Italian marquis. His mother was lady-in-waiting to Philip II of Spain, the most splendid monarch of the day. Luigi, an eldest son, was destined to be a ruler of men. He could barely walk when he got his first suit of armour. From the age of seven, though, his mind was set on other things. God became overwhelmingly real to him. He wished to be a priest. His father was furious.

In the face of opposition, Luigi steeled his resolve. He adopted penitential practices that strike us, now, as extreme. Not for nothing did he later say, 'I am a piece of twisted iron'. At length, his father let him enter the Society of Jesus, writing to the General: 'I give into your Reverence's hands the most precious thing I possess in all the world.'[102] The rest of Luigi's life is quickly recited. He began his novitiate in Rome, was named Aloysius, and did as he was told. In 1591, plague broke out. Aloysius nursed the sick, contracted the disease, and died, aged 23. His life was a flash of lightning, illumining the night sky for a moment with vast force, then disappearing. He was a man of so many parts, of resolve and generosity. What good he might have done, had he been given time! God ordained otherwise. He found him ripe, and picked him.

The feast of St Aloysius is an opportunity to reflect on the design of providence in his life – and in ours. Often, we think we have to do this, achieve that, get such and such recognition, when none of it matters. What alone matters is to give all, to live unreservedly, with great love, and to let God use our lives as he knows best, whether it is to live, work and prosper or to embrace sickness and death. Whatever our part, may it be for God's greater glory.

22 JUNE: ST JOHN FISHER AND ST THOMAS MORE

St Charles Borromeo, we know, kept a portrait of John Fisher in his study, long before the latter was canonized. This is significant, given that Borromeo was a key mover in an enterprise of church reform and that our own day's Church, too, has ready recourse to a language of reform with regard to Catholic practice and structures now. What made John Fisher a model for renewal in the sixteenth century? What can we learn from him?

First, he was a man of integrity. Even his enemies had to admit that fact. To be integral is to be whole, of a piece. We know how hard it is to be thus, torn as we are by conflicting interests within and without. The example of Fisher is as relevant as ever. Second, Fisher was a man of learning. His mind was brilliant, his learning respected throughout Europe. He never stopped being a student. His library remained for him a loved sanctuary. Thus, when presented with difficult questions, he was well equipped to give cogent, well-reasoned, persuasive answers. That, too, is an ability the Church needs in every age. Third, he was a pastoral man. He remained Bishop of Rochester, the poorest diocese in England, for over thirty years, even though he had ample scope for preferment. He had been entrusted with a specific flock; he was not minded to abandon it. Contemporaries testify that he would spend hours at a deathbed in smoke-filled hovels while his chaplain had to step outside to breathe. To use a current expression, he was a shepherd who smelt of sheep. Fourth, Fisher was a man of prayer, a devout man. Erasmus, his good friend, recognized in him real greatness of soul. Fisher lived what he taught. He had an ardent love, at once affective and intelligent, of Christ our Lord. That, too, is a quality to which we aspire timelessly. Fifth, John Fisher was a man of conscience. Were he not, he would not have been a martyr. It is this aspect of his life that makes him stand out above all. It makes him at once attractive and awe-inspiring.

Fisher was unafraid to say in no unclear terms what was truth and what was falsehood. In a sermon from 1526 he fulminated against those heretics who 'subvert the Church of Christ.' 'If we shall sit still', he went on, 'and let them in every place sow their ungracious heresies, and everywhere destroy the souls which were so dearly bought with that most precious blood of our saviour Christ Jesu, how terribly shall he lay this until our charge, when we shall be called until a reckoning for this matter?'[103] How do we hear such statements today? We are children of times that largely refuse the existence of absolute values. Claiming to be accommodating, they are in fact, ever more, times of coercion. Freedom of conscience cannot always be taken for granted.

Fisher and More were not fixated, ideological men. They were loyal citizens, friends of the king, an integral part of a social fabric they appreciated and enjoyed. Yet there came a point when the pressure put on them to deny core convictions, to call black white, cold hot, was more than they could bear. Because they *were*, both of them, whole men, men of learning, prayer and charity, they did not have it in them to renounce what they knew to be true. They held truth dear enough to die for it. They died not only for themselves, but for their friends, to keep them true. As our society turns ever more against what we stand for as Christians, we, like St Charles Borromeo, would do well to keep Fisher's countenance before our eyes often. Who knows when the hour will come for us to say 'Enough!' if we would not deny our faith and even forfeit our souls, so dearly ransomed?

9 AUGUST: ST TERESA BENEDICTA OF THE CROSS (EDITH STEIN)

Edith Stein was outstanding for her intelligence, courage, virtuous life and heroic death. In more ways than one, she personified the fate of Europe in the first half of the twentieth century. Yet for all her claims to distinction, when I think of her, I think above all of two in themselves inconspicuous incidents. They fascinate me. I sense they reveal the essential truth of this remarkable woman.

The first occurred in the Carmel of Cologne. One day, Edith was called to the parlour to see a young woman who had been among her students at Speyer, the school in which she taught after her conversion. The two chatted amiably, then parted. The woman went home, moved.

Afterwards, in a letter, she wrote that, at Speyer, all the girls had admired Edith but had been in awe of her. She had struck them as so formidable, so aloof, that they had feared to approach her. 'Yet now', she wrote, 'that I saw you again in Carmel, you were different. Somehow you have become ... maternal.' In her answer, Edith simply said: 'Each of us is called to reach full stature in Christ. This had to come, too.'[104]

The second incident occurred during the war. Edith had been moved to the Carmel of Echt, in Holland. Her superiors hoped that, there, she would be less exposed. She had, however, as a Jew, to report in person to the occupying forces. Turning up at HQ in Maastricht, she was struck by its ordinariness. It was just a busy office like any other busy office, full of girls with typewriters, their minds half on the work in hand, half on their evening engagement. The bureaucracy of evil can seem deceptively innocuous. Edith's discomfort grew while she waited. It reached its pitch when she was summoned to appear before officers of the Gestapo, whose standard greeting was, 'Heil Hitler!' Edith promptly declared, 'Praised be Jesus Christ!' She later told her prioress she knew this response could be perceived as an outright provocation, but she could do nothing else. Then and there, she said, she was intensely conscious of being caught up in the age-old battle between Jesus and Lucifer.[105]

I pray we shall likewise have the wisdom to recognize the terms of this battle, the courage to step forward to the front when we are called, the grace to let Jesus work his victory through us. For his strength is made perfect in our weakness if only we place that weakness unreservedly at his disposal.

11. Edith Stein before and after she entered monastic life: the same, yet different.

15 AUGUST: THE ASSUMPTION OF OUR LADY

The dogma of the Assumption of the Mother of God into heaven was defined by Pius XII on 1 November 1950. Outside the Catholic Church, and in some circles within, the pope's constitution *Munificentissimus Deus* was greeted with incredulity. What was going on? The year 1950 saw the first TV remote control. It was the year of *Annie Get Your Gun*, of *Sunset Boulevard*. The credit card was born in 1950, as was Stevie Wonder. And here was the Church making statements about things purported to have happened mystically to the Blessed Virgin Mary 1,900 years ago! Protestant critics thought the dogma a hodgepodge of fairy-tales, not just unbiblical but *anti*-biblical. Established thinkers like Barth and Niebuhr decried what they saw as papal arrogance. Fears were voiced that Catholics worldwide were lapsing into mother-goddess paganism. Everyone's worst suspicions seemed to be confirmed. Catholics concerned about Christian unity – a growing number – experienced trepidation.

I can't help thinking that the dogma's hysterical critics didn't in fact read *Munificentissimus Deus*. I did (I confess) only recently. I recommend you read it, too. You will find it breathes serenity, is responsibly argued, and bears the imprint of profound humility. Infallible statements are not often thought of as 'humble' – but just think for a minute what it is to stand up before the world in God's name and say, 'This is truth'. Who wouldn't tremble? The pope points out that the Assumption is no new dogma. The Church was not saying something different from what it had said before. It explicitly defined what it had always held as truth. The pope did not act off his own bat. In 1946, he wrote to every bishop in the world to seek counsel. The response was overwhelmingly affirmative. In addition, petitions poured in from every corner of the earth from the ordinary faithful. This may seem extraordinary – until, again, we insert the definition into the context of history.

In 1950, the Second World War was still an open, weeping wound. Auschwitz and Belsen were in macabre operation just yesterday. The world's supposedly Christian nations had butchered each other more horribly, more massively, than ever. There was no guarantee that things would get better. In 1950, the Korean War began; the first hydrogen bomb was made; Einstein warned that nuclear war could destroy all life. The founding of the Warsaw Pact caused dark shadows to descend again over Europe. It was easy to despair of man. In Christian souls a cry rose up, 'Lord, save us!' Men yearned to *see* God's salvation.

Eyes were raised to behold – what? 'A woman adorned with the sun, and on her head, a crown of twelve stars.'

Far from being a pious yarn, a holy-card romance, the Assumption, as dogma, is lodged in flesh and blood, in the sweat and tears of our human condition. It is thoroughly realistic. First, it points to the realism of the incarnation. God cannot pass corporeally on earth without leaving traces. To have borne God into the world is no trivial matter. Think how we venerate objects connected with the saints, certain that something of the grace that changed their lives remains still in what they handled. Think how the bodies of saints are often found to be incorrupt, rendered resistant, it would seem, to decay for having been touched by divine power. How many million times must we multiply the potency of such examples to fathom what she must have been, and remained, who bore God in her womb for nine months? Mary proves that the redemption Christ wrought is real. She is no half-angel, no pastel-coloured plaster-cast. She's real. She's one of us. She was conceived sinless, but not by some exclusive, private merit. The Immaculate Conception, the Church teaches, anticipates the salvation Jesus Christ won for all. The power that transformed the Virgin's life and death is the power that can transform ours, too, if we would let it. The Mother of God is humanity's trail-blazer. She goes ahead like a fearless explorer, showing us where we must go, what we are called to become.

In the 1940s, the cataclysmic destruction wrought by man's presumption made Christian souls long to be reminded of these facts. People were hungry for substantial food. They wanted concrete reassurance that sin will not have the last word, that death *has* been overcome, that the deepest, truest longings of the human heart – for life, love and joy, for the splendour of truth – are substantial, and will be fulfilled. They wished to be told that God *has* saved our world; that no human violence can invalidate this work.

In response to this call out of the depths, the dogma of the Assumption was defined, affirming magisterially that she who had, with perfect freedom, become Life's living tabernacle could not be held a prisoner of death. When we, you and I, look around us today, the darkness seems thicker still, in some respects, than it did in 1950. We have cause to give thanks, then, for the message of this glorious feast and to hold fast to it with all our strength. The challenge is to live in a way that is worthy of what we believe.

20 AUGUST: ST BERNARD OF CLAIRVAUX

Today's readings celebrate wisdom. Wisdom is an attribute that, now, isn't thought to be snappy. You would not put 'Aspiring to wisdom' on your CV. It would indicate reticence, boxed thinking. Spin doctors have no liking for the term. They don't say of a state leader, 'She is wise' or 'He loves wisdom'; rather, 'She is tough', or, 'He gets what he wants.' Our criteria for enterprise have become mercenary. In the ancient world, life was mercenary, too; yet wisdom was held in regard.

The later books of the Hebrew Bible are intensely preoccupied with wisdom. They offer timeless counsel on how we might become wise. They also set their sights higher. The wisdom on which they muse is increasingly the wisdom of God, the King of kings. They see this wisdom, not merely as a quality describing divine action but as part of God's being. Wisdom with a capital 'W' becomes a name for God. It is here, in such passages, that Christ, the eternal Word, is most clearly prefigured in the Old Testament, as if the Sages felt him near, espied his features from afar. Thus, when our first reading (Ecclesiasticus 15.1-6) describes how a God-fearer will come to Wisdom, it does not merely indicate prospects for self-improvement. It speaks of a living encounter.

To be prepared for Wisdom's embrace takes time. God is Truth. Wisdom displays that Truth. To reach it, we must be established in the truth. In monastic tradition, such progress in truth is described as growth in humility. To be humble is to own the reality about myself, to be fully me, without pretending to be more. It's to know who I am, what I've been, what I'm called to become. It's to bid farewell, once for all, to illusions of grandeur. A cursory look at the saint we celebrate today, whom we rejoice to claim as our patron, might cause us to ask: was Bernard a humble saint? Was his path to Wisdom humility's path? When we consider him, we find him so utterly confident, so eloquent, strong in action, often fierce in judgement. He was formidable; in his day, the most famous man in Europe. And yet those who knew and loved him well testify that he was a man of rare humility. The paradox is real.

It is illuminated for us by Bernard's first biographer, describing a crisis the saint went through early on in his monastic life. As a young abbot, Bernard was aflame with 'a maternal love for all mankind'. He saw what urgent work there was to do in the Church. He eagerly wanted to perform great things. Thereby 'desire and humility were at odds'. Not only did he overestimate his own strength; he asked too much of his brethren. Such was his aura that 'he frightened away almost all those among whom he was coming to live as abbot'. Instead of feeling drawn to him as to a source of life, they felt repulsed. Bernard, whom grace had preserved from some of the heart's most devious temptations, was horrified to learn of the squalid inner battles many monks had to fight. He spoke to them harshly, to the point of '[seeming] to sow seeds of despair in men already weak'. Like Adam in Eden, he presumed that a graced state of pure divine gift was somehow his by right, entitling him to judge less favoured men. With time, though, transformation came upon him.

It was wrought by his brethren's fidelity. For although the abbot scourged them with words, they went on entrusting themselves to him, treating him as a father even though he didn't behave like one. Their love made Bernard wake up. He 'began to question the righteousness of his indignation'. He saw that, for knowing much about heavenly things, he scarcely knew the human heart. This ignorance had caused him to sin against charity. In 'a state of turmoil', he withdrew into solitude to 'wait on the Lord'. God's mercy 'was not slow in coming to his aid'. How? It showed Bernard what he was not. It taught him to see the otherness of Wisdom, deigning to come to him as a guest, through no merit of his own. He learnt to distinguish between his own voice and the voice of the Spirit speaking in him. Having seen himself first as an agent in God's service, he grasped that, in fact, he was but an instrument, useless in itself, though capable of much when freely surrendered into God's hand.

From that time, we are told, Bernard gained new insight into God's Word. What is more, he experienced 'new sympathy with the poor and needy, the repentant sinner and the seeker after grace'. Humbled by his brothers' faithfulness and by Wisdom's condescension, he came to acquire that true humility which knows that all is gift, all is grace; that of ourselves we've no claim to anything. When later he was called into the limelight of the world, to adopt trenchant positions in matters both ecclesiastical and political, Bernard never forgot this lesson. The forbidding orator remained at the same time a meek comforter of the afflicted. Trusting God, he was cautious about himself. By owning who he was in truth, and who God truly is, he had 'come to Wisdom'. With her, he found 'gladness and joy'. Thus he could dispense these gifts also to others. The trajectory he followed, from presumption through humility to Wisdom, is essentially ours, too, to follow faithfully, in trust, with love, praying for discernment to know what is truly wise, what isn't.[106]

30 AUGUST: STS MARGARET CLITHEROW, ANN LINE AND MARGARET WARD

But for the outrageous strictures of Elizabethan legislation, the three women we commemorate today would probably have remained unknown to us; for, being tightly woven into the fabric of history, they would have been indistinguishable as individuals. As it is, they stand before us like cut, polished diamonds, all the more brilliant for being set in sackcloth.

There is a clarity to their convictions, to the courage with which they kept them, that is deeply impressive, all the more so since many of their contemporaries readily settled for compromise of one kind or another. The sort of stature they display doesn't come about overnight. It is conquered over time. Ann Line first forfeited all inherited advantage by becoming a Catholic in her late teens. She lost everything again when her husband Roger was imprisoned for recusancy, then forced to leave England for Flanders, where he died a pauper. Yet not only did she keep the faith; she was faithful with a sort of extravagance that finds scriptural resonance in Mary Magdalene's ointment jar. Before being hanged at Tyburn on 27 February 1601, Ann exclaimed: 'I am sentenced to die for harbouring a Catholic priest, and so far am I from repenting for having so done, that I wish, with all my soul, that where I have entertained one, I could have entertained a thousand!'[107] She faced death, witnesses said, with 'not the least commotion or change in her countenance'.[108]

Such examples inspire our own exercise in discipleship. They give us courage, should we feel tempted to despair at the state of the Church today, for they teach us that the Church's holiness is not always most in evidence where we would most readily expect, and hope, to find it. The seed of sanctity grows in secret; what matters is the goodness of the soil. Christ does not abandon the Church – but he may manifest himself within it in unlikely places. We have to be watchful, then, and strive to recognize him even now where he chooses to be found.

15 SEPTEMBER: THE SORROWS OF THE VIRGIN MARY

When I was growing up, a woman in our neighbourhood died. She seemed to me old at the time. She was probably about the age I am now. My family did not know her well, but we did see a lot of her mother, who bore her loss with stoic calm, though a depth of grief would sometimes seep through her defences. I remember being struck by something I heard her utter: 'It just isn't *right*, it isn't in the nature of things: I should have gone first!'

The pain of a mother at the death of her child is unconscionable. It confronts us with an open wound before which we can only incline ourselves in silence.

That is what we do today, as we recall the sorrows of the Blessed Virgin Mary. Again and again, with maternal perseverance, the Church recalls us to the human truth and density of God's incarnation. We need the reminders. Reared on theology and catechetics, we are accustomed to think of the Passion of Christ as 'propitiation' and 'atonement'. These are true, necessary notions. But may they never obscure the human reality of a Mother's Son condemned to death! May our high spirituality never take the edge off a middle-aged woman's tears of desolation as her heart was wrenched apart!

The texts of today's Mass speak of compassion. We hear of Mary's compassion; that is, of her 'suffering with' Jesus. But claims are made, too, on our compassion. Let us remember the Lord's word: 'He who hears my words and does them is my brother and sister and mother' (Mark 3.35). We are, each of us, called to stand in Mary's stead. We are called, with her, to stand by the cross in darkness. We believe, we know, that that darkness will be turned to light, of course. But we must still enter it as darkness. Today we are invited to ponder this fact in quiet recollection. Our hearts as a result are made vulnerable to Christ's overwhelming love. The rocky ground of our soul is pierced, for living water to gush forth to transform our desert into an oasis.

1 OCTOBER: ST THÉRÈSE

The attitude that should mark our response to God's design in our lives, says St Thérèse, is abandonment to God's providence.[109] But that is not all. We must live this attitude with audacity. We are to abandon ourselves with daring.[110] It is good to be reminded that surrender to God is no mere resignation. It is no weary consent to some fatalistic scheme. It is deliberate forward movement, calling for courage.

What matters is to *will* God's will, to dive into it like a swimmer dives into the sea from the pier, and to take this plunge deliberately, with grace. I was recently helped to understand what this might mean when reading a life of Marthe Robin. This extraordinary woman, a source of consolation to thousands, was once sought out by the philosopher Jean Guitton at a time when he bore a grief so intense it appeared to crush him. He was paralysed by a broken heart at the death of his wife. Marthe gave him the following advice: 'When in this sort of state, you must throw yourself onto God with all your strength. To do this is more than just action. It is abandonment.' *C'est plus que de l'action, c'est de l'abandon.*[111]

Abandonment is not opposed to action. It is action in transcendent form, raised up to a higher level. It happens when our natural strength has run its course, when we begin, almost despite ourselves, for sheer necessity, to respond *super*naturally. At such graced times we know from experience that it is true: 'It *is* when I am weak that I am strong' (2 Corinthians 12.10). We cast ourselves forward with a strength we do not have – and then find that it carries, raises us up, causing us to soar, transforming constraint into a state of boundless, strangely joyful freedom. St Thérèse is our guide on this royal path, strewing its apparent roughness with roses. We are summoned to follow in her footprints trustingly, audaciously, today and every day.

1 NOVEMBER: ALL SAINTS

How many times have we not heard people make remarks like, 'I am no saint, of course', before they go on to tear apart somebody else? Perhaps we have done it ourselves. Sainthood can seem impossibly remote from the reality of our lives. It ought not to. John Paul II, that indefatigable canonizer, proclaimed a host of new saints with a clear catechetical purpose: he wanted us, the people of God, to realize that the Church's catalogue of saints comprises men and women from every walk of life, of every shape and size, men and women very like ourselves. He wanted that realization to prompt a question. If it could happen to them, why not to me? He wanted us to have spiritual ambition – and now, there he is, himself a saint!

The notion of sainthood as something familiar and close is no news to readers of the New Testament letters. St Paul is positively promiscuous in his use of the term 'saint'. Left, right and centre he calls upon the 'saints' of this church or that. Not that he thought them all perfect in Christian stature. But he recognized in them that divine potential which makes an aspiration to sanctity not only licit but mandatory. Think of the prologue to 1 Corinthians: 'To the church of God that is in Corinth, to those sanctified in Christ Jesus, called to be saints.' How about substituting 'Whitwick' for 'Corinth'? Are we prepared for the challenge?

I say 'challenge', though of course sanctity is not something we achieve. It is pure gift from beginning to end. Yet it is a gift we must be disposed to receive. Our will and our desire have their necessary part to play. God calls each of us to be a saint. But he will not force us. We do not have to enjoy beatitude. We can opt out of communion with God. The call to be a saint comes in the form of an invitation. Almighty God, the creator of heaven and earth, approaches us with something like the modesty of a little child, a child who has not yet learnt to dissimulate the stirrings of the heart, and has the courage to say: 'Do you want to be my friend?' Such is the humility of our God. Such is the nature of his love.

He has lavished it upon us, that love. He has made us his sons and daughters. In Christ, he pours his grace out upon us continually. Just think how enormous all this is! Think what an extraordinary message we get from today's liturgy! God has given us everything we need to know him, to love him, and – astonishingly – to be like him, to see him as he is. How have we received his gifts? How are we going to receive them today, here and now? This great feast commemorates the countless multitudes who have had the courage, love and longing to open their lives entirely to God's love and to be transformed by it. We are called to join their company. Next time we are tempted to say, 'Of course, I am no saint', let us stop in our tracks, swallow our words, remember Jesus Christ, and ask ourselves: 'Well, why not?'

2 NOVEMBER: ALL SOULS

We shall all die. We shall all reach the day when, alone, we must abandon what, through life, we have acquired, reduced to what we *are*. Dying manifests what, by living, we've become. Death may come gradually, at the end of a long life. It may come unexpectedly. We know neither the day nor the hour. But it will come.

Given the certainty, the universality of death, it is remarkable that, now, people widely collude in an effort to pretend that death does not exist. Dying is all but invisible in Western society. It is considered indecent to refer to it. We can't bear the powerlessness of it. By a strange paradox, it seems to me that the ongoing debate about assisted dying is, in reality, tied up with our postmodern denial of death. We wish to be in charge to the last. We wish to nurture the illusion that we're masters of our destiny. And so we wish to abolish the waiting for death. We prefer to flick the switch when it suits us, when we've had enough of the performance.

A Christian testimony is nowhere more telling than in the way we face death. To a Christian, death is no black hole, no brick wall, no absorbing oblivion. To a Christian, death is an encounter. We are not the victims of death. Death is something we perform. It is a task, the culmination of our Christian lives. We enact it as we abandon ourselves, with confidence and trust, to the 'everlasting arms' that have carried us, we know, all the way we have walked, and that will bear us still when we can walk no longer. Today's commemoration is a confession of hope. It proclaims, indeed it celebrates, the dignity of death, its paschal character. By the Easter mystery, grief at parting is tempered by the joy of meeting.

Yet All Souls' Day is still more. We are reminded that although we must die on our own, each for himself or for herself, we are not abandoned in dying or in death. Our incorporation into Christ, manifest in our belonging to the Church, sustains us into the grave and beyond. This praying unity remains intact when our heart of flesh stops beating. We are part of a communion of charity that has no bounds. Death is a mere episode in a shared, redemptive story that continues without interruption.

On this day, we pray with fervour and with peace for the dead who have gone before us. And we take comfort from the fact that we, too, shall one day be raised up and supported by the Church's unceasing intercession. Love is stronger than death, a great deal stronger. Many waters cannot quench it (cf. Song of Songs 8.7).

30 NOVEMBER: ST ANDREW

Modern psychology has taught us much about sibling rivalry, believed to be among the primary relations that form a life, with the potential to really mess it up. Research gleaned from the analyst's couch is corroborated by Scripture. Think of Cain and Abel, Jacob and Esau, Leah and Rachel. What twistedness, what pain, we see in these pairs of brothers and sisters! It is interesting, then, that in recruiting for the apostolic college, seeking heads for the Twelve Tribes of the New Israel, Christ should have wished a high percentage – one-third – to be blood brothers.

The two accounts we have of the call of Andrew and Peter suggests that even this pair had moments of difference. In John's Gospel, Andrew is the first to follow Jesus; only through his intermediacy is Peter dragged along. Meanwhile, in Matthew (who builds on Mark, Peter's disciple) the two are called together, with Peter named first as a matter of course. Did Peter and Andrew, like James and John, squabble about who was greater? If they did not, their followers did, and the complex dynamic of brothers is evident to this day in the relationship between the Petrine See of Rome and the See of Constantinople, which traces its origin back to St Andrew.

If Christ assumed these complications into his closest band of followers, it was perhaps to show that natural limitations, relational conditioning, can be overcome if we truly become disciples. James and John, Peter and Andrew, grow in faith and stature through the Gospel account, to the extent that, after Christ's rising, they are ready to be sent, each with his itinerary, to the ends of the earth, to proclaim life's victory. They've grown up. They've left themselves behind. Thus they're free for mission. The death to self to which a Christian is called is about more than just mortification. It is a process of liberation, enabling us to put old complexes and rivalries to rest in order to strain forward, out of darkness into light.

This is a message put before us on this feast. In the concluding prayer of the Mass, we pray for strength 'that by the example of the Blessed Apostle Andrew, we, who carry in our body the death of Christ, may merit to live with him in glory'. St Andrew's life culminated in an oblation that emulated Christ's glorious sacrifice. His heart had been made wide. His love had been set free. He could give all. We are called to follow in his footsteps. We are bold enough to greet that invitation with a confident, grateful, faithful 'Amen!'

3 DECEMBER: ST FRANCIS XAVIER

Francis Xavier was a student in Paris when, in 1530, he got a roommate he didn't care for, a Basque called Ignatius Loyola. It is not clear what eventually led Francis to sign up to Ignatius's apostolic project. Ignatius would later say that Francis Xavier was 'the toughest dough he'd ever had to knead'.[112] Once Francis's mind was made up, though, he was unshakeable. He was one of the seven companions who, on 15 August 1534, gave themselves to God at Montmartre, vowing to place their lives at the disposal of the pope for the service of the Gospel. Francis worked in Goa, the Spice Islands and Japan. He died in 1552, preparing to launch a mission in China.

Francis Xavier's ministry was not one of constant success. A telling incident occurred in 1551. Having spent two years in Japan, Francis had experienced only failure. His mission to Kyoto had been a flop, so he retired to Yamaguchi. After several months' effort without making a single convert, Francis's companion Fernandez was teaching in public one day when a man came up and spat in his face. Fernandez calmly wiped his face, and continued preaching. Faced with this spectacle, one of the Jesuits' bitterest enemies converted to the faith and asked for baptism. Within a few weeks the local Church counted many converts.[113]

We're given to complaining, today, that society does not want to hear the Christian message. What is it, though, that niggles us? Is it that Christ is unknown? Or is it our sense that no one appreciates us and our once-prestigious institutions? Often our motives are mixed. Therefore it is important to examine them.

Francis Xavier was a man unconcerned with status and appearance. When he got his call to the East, his only baggage was 'two pairs of trousers and a cassock beyond description'. He set off as a poor man to preach the poor Christ to the poor. Throughout his life he stayed poor. He was invulnerable to humiliation because he had no face to lose. He was driven by compassion for unbelievers and an ardent love of Christ. It is good that we should measure our commitment against the example of such a disciple. We, too, in our way, are called to cast fire upon the earth. Let's make sure our hearts are set on doing just that, not on restoring tatty Christmas lights to adorn our own houses. If the world spits on us, our response may reveal the face of Christ in a way more effective than any preaching. The Lord exhorts us, 'You received without charge, give without charge' (Matthew 10.8). So that is what we must do.

Appendix

This conference was given to the General Chapter of the Order of Cistercians of the Strict Observance in the summer of 2014, in response to an invitation from the Abbot General, Dom Eamon Fitzgerald, and his council.

VISION

The letter inviting me to give this address instructed me: 'write a paper [...] on <u>your</u> vision of the Order for the 21st century'. The pronoun was underlined. I will speak in subjective terms, then, from within my frame of reference: such is my brief. My topic is a vision *of* the Order *for* the twenty-first century, not *for* the Order *of* the twenty-first century. I take this to mean that I should speak of what I see when I look at the Order. It makes sense. Any future vision depends on an appraisal of the status quo. To establish it, we must speak, and listen, to each other.

A vision presupposes a point of view. In this assembly, I am a worker of the eleventh hour. Many of you, if not most, have been monks and nuns since before I was born. You can trace patterns I cannot perceive. From this I have much to learn. What *I* can do, I suppose, is to offer a different kind of retrospect, the vision of one more recently arrived of what has been passed on to him. In so doing, I feel gratitude. I also feel perplexity. My perplexity springs from what I see as a crisis of transmission. It is on this I wish to reflect.

When I entered the monastery in 2002, I was conscious of entering a flow of continuous life. I was no less conscious of entering a history of rupture. The story was told anecdotally daily. Most aspects of observance and liturgy invited comparison with former times, which for some, I gathered, represented a primitive stage in monastic evolution, when the law had not yet been tempered by grace; others spoke of it as a lost Eden barred by fiery swords. Whatever the emotional charge of 'now' and 'then', the gap was evident. The decree of unification had altered the community's structure; the redefinition of silence alongside the abandonment of dormitories and scriptoria had affected the nature of fraternal relations; liturgical life had been comprehensively reimagined; evolving positions in theology had recast the very nature of Cistercian life. People had come and gone, not just in the novitiate and juniorate.

From 1950 to today, our community has seen 60 solemn professions. In the same period, 30 brethren in solemn vows have left monastic life. Even the topography of the house is eloquent. Hardly a room functions now as it did 50 years ago. For a novice, the sea change was bewildering. Amid such upheaval, which were the lines of continuity that mattered? Much that was branded 'tradition' went no further back than to fraught community meetings of the 1960s, when the brethren were often divided down the middle, with changes introduced *ad experimentum*, to placate the aggrieved.

At this point, let me be clear: I am not attempting to introduce some artificial (and tedious) dichotomy between pre- and post-conciliar Catholicism. Even less do I position myself on a spectrum from 'conservative' to 'liberal'. Tottering as I am on the brink of stolid middle age, I am too old to be charged with the romantic nostalgia supposed to afflict today's youth. What I see affecting us is a hub of issues that is cultural rather than theological. Ringing in my mind is an English monk's journalistic account of monastic life in the 1960s. It speaks of the Spirit then making all things new, acting 'like a cruise missile'.[114]

For being racy, the expression captures a mood felt by many. A cruise missile leaves great emptiness behind. The possibilities inherent in this void engendered vast creative efforts. These were coloured by their time, an exceptional time, in the hope of making an ancient tradition speak contemporary language. Lasting achievements were made relationally, spiritually, intellectually. But certain adjustments show their age. Many texts, tunes, interior designs and community manifestos that may have seemed 'relevant' then appear touchingly antiquated now, monuments to the ephemeral. If they are still with us, it is not least because our recruitment has, for a half-century, been sporadic at best: within our microcosm, sensibilities have remained fairly constant. Further, time-bound forms have perdured on account of the titanic effort that went into them.

In my monastery, there was, by the time of colour TV's triumph in society at large, a pronounced creativity-fatigue. The brethren were dizzy with change, tired of talk about change, wounded by conflicts change had caused. They wanted things to stay as they were. When I entered, I encountered a palpable anxiety. The message was clear: 'Don't tamper with things, don't re-release the furies!'

I honour the good wrought by *aggiornamento*: the review of over-meticulous usages; the shedding of liturgical accretions; the strengthening of fraternal bonds; the fostering of sound conversation; the divulgation of our literary patrimony. I am moved by the intention to renew our life that it might be a sign to our times. Yet hopes for a new spring have, for many of us, been unfulfilled. We find ourselves in a state that is decidedly autumnal. There are complex reasons for this. But surely there are questions we must ask, given the scope of the reform in whose wake we sail. Which of its accomplishments are transient, which timeless? How does this graced but trying, by intervals euphoric and tormented, endeavour fit into a longer narrative of shared identity? What have we become?

I know that, to some, such questions seem an outright provocation. But I do not ask them to provoke, much less to offend. I ask because I need an answer. When I consider our heritage, I feel frankly overwhelmed by a paradigm of interpretation I often cannot follow because it rests, ultimately, on an unsharable experience: on having been there at the time. The last generation who *was* there is gracefully fading away. How do we latter-born make *our* return *ad fontes* in order to take our charism into the future? This, to me, is a burningly practical concern. With it in mind, I offer some thoughts on what strikes me when I look at what has been handed on to me.

A. First, I note a passage from idealism to
   pragmatism. Monasticism, like other institutions,
   defined itself in the mid-nineteenth century
   by rigorous first principles on the basis of
   which material, experiential phenomena were

defined. A century's experience of absolutisms made this approach as unpalatable in the cloister as elsewhere. Reflecting on itself, a community such as mine came to ask rather: what meets our needs? What can we manage? What helps us? These were timely questions. Yet the more they are brought to the fore, the vaguer our sense of finality becomes. Caught up in where we are now, we may lose our sense of where we are going.

B. This prompts a second observation, of a referential change from objective to subjective criteria. A confrère used to relay what his novice master told him in the late 1940s: 'Keep the Rule and up you go!' The saying occasioned mirth. It was meant to show up a primitive legalism consisting of rubrics and regulations. We were told that we, by contrast, enjoyed a charismatic freedom to listen to the Spirit. I share this Pentecostal expectation, yet a paradox befuddles me: when did Spirit and Rule come to stand in opposition? Such narrative discontinuity poses special problems in the lineage of Cîteaux, which has been described – to my mind brilliantly – as an aspiration to pursue 'the spirit that only the authentic letter can set free'.[115]

C. As a function of the two factors named, I am struck by a shift of emphasis from *praxis* to spirituality. It presents itself in banal ways. In our community, we are quite muddled, now, about ordinary ritual: what counts as right comportment in regular places and common exercises? How do we move *together*? No one is certain. For decades we have had no norms.

There was an allergy to codes of conduct; a warning not to fix on externals and to focus instead on the spirit within. I observe that this shift can be corrosive of shared identity.

I observe, too, that many monks, the young not least, find our mystical tradition and patrology difficult to access. They yearn to be given something to *do*. I do not think this springs from crypto-Pelagianism. I think it evidences a desire for a whole life that engages both soul *and* body, a yearning to see oneness emerge from multiplicity.

D. This evokes a tendency I would call centrifugal. If I may refer again to our community: we have had to work hard to recover basic elements of common life such as daily chapter, shared *lectio* and mental prayer, a culture of shared meals. This unifying work was conducted in the teeth of a scattering trend, evident even in the way our abbey had come to be organized: nothing much went on in the middle; life happened on the periphery. This caused vitality to drain from the *corpus monasterii*. For life to thrive, it seems essential to consolidate the centre.

The ultimate centre of our life is Christ, of course. A crucial objective has been to 'start afresh' from him. This is wonderful, as long as we do not construct our calling in too generic terms, losing sight of Christ's embodiment in forms that are peculiarly our own. Pains have been taken to inculturate our life, be the culture in question simply that of our own community. This, too, is good, as long as we beware of too subjective renderings. In the climate of today, may one risk forgetting that monastic life in each generation is received, not created?

Our Fathers stressed the outward expression of inner values. They believed in the power of observance to foster identity and safeguard unity. I perceive that our life has become more formless than it was. I note that we no longer speak readily of observance as 'form'. What we do speak about a lot is the need for more formation. But how can we form people to a form that is elastic to the point of sometimes becoming diffuse? Abbot Cuthbert Butler once commented on the elasticity of Benedictine life. It is a 'very good term', he conceded, then added:

> elastic, unless it is worn out, ever tends, as the pressure of [external] forces wanes, to return to its original condition, and when the forces cease to operate, it does re-assume its native form. It is in this property that elasticity lies, and that elastic differs from putty.[116]

My sense is that ours is a time of such release of pressure. I consider the return to form a primary challenge – an exciting, joyful challenge! Fifty years ago, the Order was intensely aware of being caught up in renewal. Dom J.-B. Porion, O.Cart. wrote of an encounter with an unnamed member of the OCSO in November 1967. He summed it up as follows: 'They believe that, through an unprecedented explosion of grace, the charism of the founders is now as widely available as the ability to drive a motorcar.'[117]

Our present self-confidence is probably more modest. The task, meanwhile, is no less great: to produce from our treasury things both new and old; to build bridges where connections have been lost; to rekindle our Fathers' faith in the Benedictine Rule's orientation and tools as a sure way to union with Christ; to affirm that this unifying process acquires uniquely lovely features from our patrimony, which is not only literary, but composed of chant, ritual, architecture, agriculture, and an art of forming a living communion in harmony and beauty, ardently contemplative, 'with no *discord* in our conduct, [...] by one charity, one Rule, and like usages'.[118] Thus we shall be equipped for our mission in the Church. May our sights be set high, our longing be profound, our outlook be well thought-out and hospitable. Such would be my vision. Forgive me for not being able to account for it more briefly.

Notes on the Text

All translations are mine, except when otherwise noted. Scripture is generally cited from the RSV, but I have sometimes made adjustments based on the original texts. The Psalms are referenced according to the numbering of the Vulgate.

I have cited and referenced Augustine's *De Trinitate* and Aelred's Sermon from editions in the *Corpus Christianorum Series Latina*; the *Apophthegmata Patrum* (thematic collection), Ephrem, Athanasius, and Cassian from editions in the *Sources Chrétiennes*; the *Exordium Magnum*, Gilbert of Hoyland's sermon, and the first Life of St Bernard from Migne's *Patrologia Latina* (vols 184 and 185); Eusebius's *Ecclesiastical History* and that of Bede from the *Loeb Classical Library*; Saint Benedict's Rule from *The Rule of Saint Benedict in English*, ed. Timothy Fry and others (Collegeville, MN: The Liturgical Press, 1982); the *Exordium parvum* and the *Carta caritatis* from *Les plus anciens textes de Cîteaux*, ed. by J. Bonton and J. B. Van Damme (Achel: Abbaye cistercienne, 1974).

The story of my meeting with Emmanuel, the piece entitled 'To Let the Body Breathe', and the homily for the Ascension have been published in *The Tablet* in modified versions. They are reproduced here with the editor's gracious permission.

The figure used as a visual divider in the text is a detail from a floor tile in the chapter house at Mount Saint Bernard, a large octagonal room designed by Edward Pugin, the son of A. W., who drew the main monastery. Several symbols are wound into one. The contour of an M suggests Mary, Daughter of Zion, who enabled a new, fruitful shoot to spring forth from Jesse's old root. The medievals loved to associate the name Maria with *maria*, the plural form of *mare*, meaning 'the sea'. What the Mother of Christ represents for sailors in the Barque of Peter, often exposed to rough waters, is apparent in the outline of an anchor. This figure evokes the space in which many texts in the book were delivered. Prostrate on the floor of that room, I made my petition to receive the monastic habit; in that room, likewise, I made my profession as a monk.

NOTES

1 Archimandrite Sophrony (Sakharov), *Starets Silouane, Moine du Mont-Athos: Vie – Doctrine – Écrits* (Sisteron: Présences, 1973), p. 47.

2 St Benedict voices the aspiration that 'in all things God may be glorified' in a passage that deals with the pricing of monastic produce for sale, so nothing is beyond glory's reach. *The Rule of Saint Benedict* (henceforth *RB*), 57.9.

3 *Hymnes sur le paradis*, 3.16.

4 I refer to a wonderful testimony spoken towards the end of Philip Gröning's largely wordless film, *Into Great Silence* (2005), when an old Carthusian sums up the insight gained through a lifetime's fidelity with these words.

5 *Vie d'Antoine*, 2.3–5.

6 *Les Apophtegmes des Pères* (henceforth *AP*), 1.3.

7 *RB*, Prologue 45.

8 *RB*, Prologue 2.

9 *RB*, Prologue 3.

10 *RB*, 4.21.

11 *'Cette règle, c'est un précis du christianisme, un docte et mystérieux abrégé de toute la doctrine de l'Évangile.'* Jacques Bénigne Bossuet, *Oraisons funèbres et panégyriques*, 2 vols (Paris: Garnier, 1872), II, 21.

12 *RB*, 4.1, 8, 9, 16, 19, 29, 31.

13 *RB*, 43.3.

14 *Constitutions of the Order of Cistercians of the Strict Observance* (Rome: Order of Cistercians of the Strict Observance, 1990), 19.1.

15 Cf. *Catechism of the Catholic Church*, n. 845.

16 *RB*, 57.9.

17 Cited in the Third Memoir, just before the epilogue. *Memorie di Suor Lucia*, assembled by Luigi Kondor (Fatima: Vice-Postulazione della Beatificazione dei veggenti, 1980), p. 112.

18 *RB*, 2.2. '*Christi enim agere vices in monasterio creditur*'. That is to say: the abbot 'holds Christ's place' in the sense of being an instrument through which Christ can act.

19 Dom Marie Gabriel Sortais, *Les Choses qui plaisent à Dieu* (Bellefontaine: Éditions de Bellefontaine, 1967), p. 145, citing Cardinal Maurice Feltin's pastoral letter for Lent 1958, a text addressed, not just to monks or religious, but to all the faithful.

20 *RB*, 64.20.

21 I am grateful to Dom Timothy Kelly, who has taught me such a lot, for these words.

22 This is brought out in chapter 71, which bears the heading, 'That the brothers should obey one another'.

23 *RB*, 9.2.

24 Letter 67 in *The Letters of Saint Bernard of Clairvaux*, trans. Bruno Scott James (Kalamazoo, MI: Cistercian Publications, 1998).

25 *AP*, 2.35.

26 *AP*, 2.2.

27 *AP*, 2.29.

28 *AP*, 2.19.

29 *Sermones in Canticum Salomonis*, 35.2.

30 *Exordium Parvum*, 9.

31 1.29. I cite Paul McGuckin's translation, published in Kalamazoo, MI, by Cistercian Publications in 1982.

32 *RB*, 22.8, 4.65f., 63.17, 71.1, 4.19.

33 'Such people as these immediately put aside their own concerns, abandon their own will, and lay down whatever they have in hand, leaving it unfinished', *RB*, 5.7f.

34 David Knowles, *The Historian and Character* (Cambridge: Cambridge University Press, 1963), p. 335.

35 '[H]oc semper in corde, sæpe etiam in ore habebat, "Bernarde, Bernarde, ad quid venisti?"'Vita Prima 1.4.19.

36 RB, 9.3.

37 Therefore St Benedict instructs that the brethren's beds 'are to be inspected frequently by the abbot, lest private possessions be found there' (RB, 55.16), an injunction I dare say most contemporary superiors interpret figuratively.

38 See chapter 62, on the priests of the monastery and chapter 63, on community rank.

39 'If a brother is sent on some errand and expects to return to the monastery that same day, he must not presume to eat outside, even if he receives a pressing invitation, unless perhaps the abbot has ordered it' (RB, 51.1f.). It is not that St Benedict begrudges the monks dinner. What he opposes is self-indulgence in stealth.

40 RB, 72.11.

41 Apostolic Letter to All Consecrated People, 21 November 2014.

42 Exordium Magnum, 4.33.

43 Letter 326, to the prior of the Charterhouse of Portes.

44 From the foundation account De Lysa, in Arne Odd Johnsen, De norske cistercienserklostre 1146–1264 (Oslo, Bergen and Tromsø: Universitetsforlaget, 1977), p. 72.

45 Constitutions, Preface.

46 A story well told by Augustin-Hervé Laffay in Dom Augustin de Lestrange et l'avenir du monachisme: 1754–1827 (Paris: Cerf, 1998).

47 This and subsequent references are taken from Edmund Sheridan Purcell, Life and Letters of Ambrose Phillips de Lisle (London and New York: Macmillan, 1900), pp. viii–ix, 70–86.

48 'Veritatem dico, fratres, non mentior. Ordo noster crux Christi est'. Sermo 10.31.

49 Printed as the first six in the Sources Chrétiennes edition of Isaac's Sermons.

50   *Practical & Theological Chapters* 3.14, here, too, in McGuckin's rendering.

51   *Phaedrus*, 246–54.

52   A Nun of Stanbrook, *In a Great Tradition: Tribute to Dame Laurentia McLachlan* (London: Murray, 1956), pp. 292f., 296.

53   *A Testimonial to Grace* (New York: Sheed & Ward, 1946).

54   *RB*, 67.5.

55   *The Spectator*, 12 July 2014.

56   *RB*, 2.4, 12.

57   *RB*, 64.9.

58   These are the words with which St Benedict's Rule begins.

59   *RB*, 64.11ff.; 27.8; 2.7, 38.

60   The prayers from the Rite of Blessing of an abbot are found in the *Pontificale Romanum*, ed. Manlio Sodi and Alessandro Toniolo (Vatican City: Libreria Editrice Vaticana, 2008).

61   *RB*, 4.39.

62   *RB*, 43.4.

63   *RB*, Prologue 19.

64   'If a disciple obeys grudgingly and murmurs, not only aloud but also in his heart, then, even though he carries out the order, his action will not be accepted with favour by God, who sees that he is murmuring in his heart' (*RB*, 5.17f.).

65   *RB*, 23.1.

66   *RB*, 34.6f.

67   *RB*, 35.13.

68   *RB*, 40.8f.

69   *RB*, 41.5; 53.18.

70   *Il Cammino del monaco*, trans. and ed. Luigi d'Ayala Valva (Bose: Qiqajon, 2009), p. 41.

71   *Conferences*, 24.6.

72   *RB*, 72.5; 36.5.

73   *RB*, Prologue 50.

74   Cited from Sr Benedicta Ward's precious volume, *Harlots in the Desert: A Study of Repentance in Early Monastic Sources* (Kalamazoo, MI: Cistercian Publications, 1987).

75 Tordis Ørjasæter, *Kjærligheten har sitt eget språk: En mors fortelling* (Oslo: Kagge, 2017), p. 147f.

76 Now available in English under the title, *A Time to Die: Monks on the Threshold of Eternal Life* (San Francisco: Ignatius, 2019).

77 *De incarnatione Verbi*, 50–1.

78 From the fifth step of the *Ladder of Divine Ascent*.

79 Recounted in the chapter 'Nuit de feu' in *Confessions d'une religieuse* (Paris: Flammarion, 2008).

80 *Letters from Baron Friedrich von Hügel to a Niece*, ed. Gwendolen Greene (London and Toronto: Dent, 1928), p. xvi.

81 *RB*, Prologue 17.

82 *The Works of Elizabeth Barrett Browning* (Ware: Wordsworth Editions, 1994), p. 499.

83 From the 1914 collection 'Responsibilities' in *Selected Poetry*, ed. A. Norman Jeffares (London: Macmillan, 1962), p. 63.

84 Elsa Morante, *Alibi* (Turin: Einaudi, 2004), p. 49.

85 The beginning of hymn 21 in *Sancti Romani Melodi Cantica*, ed. Paul Maas and C. A. Trypanis (Oxford: Clarendon Press, 1963).

86 '*Jésus sera en agonie jusqu'à la fin du monde: il ne faut pas dormir pendant ce temps-là*', *Pensée* 736 (=Brunschvicg 553) in *Oeuvres complètes de Pascal*, ed. Jacques Chevalier, Bibliothèque de la Pléiade (Paris: Gallimard, 1954).

87 *La Caverne des trésors: Les deux recensions syriaques*, ed. Su-Min Ri, Corpus Scriptorum Christianorum Orientalium 486–7, Scriptores syri, 207–8 (Louvain: Peeters, 1987), 5.3–8.

88 Thus the situation is summed up in a later, Arabic version of this Midrash: *La Caverna dei Tesori: Testo arabo con traduzione italiana e commento*, ed. A. Battista and B. Bagatti (Jerusalem: Franciscan Printing Press, 1979), p. 45.

89 George Herbert, *A Selection of his Finest Poems*, ed. Louis L. Martz, The Oxford Poetry Library (Oxford: OUP, 1994), p. 31.

90 *'Libera me, deus meus, a multiloquio quod patior intus in anima mea misera in conspectu tuo et confugiente ad misericordiam tuam.'* De Trinitate, 15.33–5.

91 The programme, broadcast on 3 September 2000, is available on the BBC website.

92 Evelyn Waugh, *Brideshead Revisited: The Sacred and Profane Memories of Captain Charles Ryder* (London: The Folio Society, 1995), p. 65.

93 Alice Develey's article, 'Jésus, Jupiter, Louis XIV ... et Emmanuel Macron', was published in *Le Figaro* on 16 June 2017.

94 Archimandrite Sophrony Sakharov, *Words of Life* (Tolleshunt Knights: Stavropegic Monastery of St John the Baptist, 1996), p. 24.

95 I have drawn on Dom Laurence Hendriks' noble account in *The London Charterhouse: Its Monks and its Martyrs* (London: Kegan Paul, Trench & Co., 1889).

96 I have rewritten in the singular the sentiment Sr Gabriella voiced in the plural to Fr Basilio Meloni on 1 February 1939: *'Sento dalle sue parole come il Signore la provi e quanto abbia a soffrire. Ci siamo offerti con la nostra consacrazione e il Signore ci ha fatto l'onore di prenderci in parola.'* Lettere dalla Trappa, ed. Mariella Carpinello (Rome: San Paolo, 2006).

97 Jacobus de Voragine, *The Golden Legend*, trans. William Granger Ryan (Princeton and Oxford: Princeton University Press, 2012), pp. 238–42.

98 *Ecclesiastical History*, 2.15.

99 From 'Life and Writings of Br. M. Rafael Barón (VII)', trans. Sr. Charles Longuemare, in *Cistercian Studies Quarterly*, 38.1 (2003), 57f.

100 I refer to the admonition Anthony gave his brethren on his deathbed: τὸν Χριστὸν ἀεὶ ἀναπνέετε, meaning literally, 'Breathe Christ in and out at all times' (*Vie d'Antoine*, 91.3).

101 *Ecclesiastical History of the English Nation*, 1.7. It is significant that Alban, when the judge asked him to account

for his ethnic and social credentials ('*cuius familiae vel generis es?*'), subverted the categories and said: 'What does it matter of which stock I am? [...] I am a Christian, and would have you know that I devote myself to Christian tasks and duties.'

102 Aloysius's view of himself and his father's letter are cited in the tenth and thirteenth chapters of Silas Henderson's *St. Aloysius Gonzaga, S.J.: With an Undivided Heart* (San Francisco: Ignatius, 2017).

103 Cited in Maria Dowling's *Fisher of Men: A Life of John Fisher 1469–1523* (London: Palgrave Macmillan, 1999), p. 91.

104 This story is told in many books about Edith Stein, and seems to be attested, but I have yet to find a reliable first-hand source.

105 Teresia Renata de Spiritu Sancto [Posselt], *Edith Stein*, trans. by Cecily Hastings and Donald Nicholl (London and New York: Sheed and Ward, 1952), p. 198.

106 *Vita Prima*, 1.5–7.

107 Richard Challoner, *Memoirs of Missionary Priests, and other Catholics of both Sexes, that Have Suffered Death in England on Religious Accounts, from the Year 1577, to 1684*, 2 vols (Philadelphia: Green, 1839), I, 235.

108 William Eusebius Andrews, *An Examination of Fox's Calendar*, 3 vols (London: Andrews, 1826), III, 112.

109 As in a letter written just before her death, on 10 August 1897, to l'abbé Bellière: '*qu'il est doux de s'abandonner entre ses bras, sans craintes ni désirs*'. Sainte Thérèse de l'Enfant-Jésus et de la Sainte Face, *Correspondance Générale*, 2 vols (Paris: Cerf, Desclée de Brouwer, 1972), II, 1061.

110 We are to nurture '*une disposition du cœur qui nous rend humbles et petits entre les bras de Dieu, conscients de notre faiblesse, et confiants jusqu'à l'audace en sa bonté de Père*'. From the *Novissima Verba* of 3 August 1897. Thérèse de Lisieux, *Oeuvres complètes* (Paris: Cerf, Desclée de Brouwer, 1996), p. 1074.

111 Bernard Peyrous, *Vie de Marthe Robin* (Paris: l'Emmanuel, 2006), p. 352.

112 Georg Schurhammer, *Francis Xavier: His Life, His Times*, trans. by M. Joseph Costelloe, 4 vols (Rome: The Jesuit Historical Institute, 1982), I, 172.

113 Ibid., IV, 156–63.

114 From Dom Simon McGurk's account in *Touched by God: Ten Monastic Journeys*, ed. Laurentia Johns (London: Burns & Oates, 2008), p. 169f.

115 A helpful insight formulated by Pauline Matarasso in her volume, *The Cistercian World: Monastic Writings of the Twelfth Century* (London: Penguin, 1993), p. 10.

116 *Benedictine Monachism: Studies in Benedictine Life and Rule*, 2nd edn, with Supplementary Notes (London and New York: Longmans, Green, and Company, 1924), p. 413.

117 '*En somme, ils croient que, par une explosion sans précédent de la grâce, le charisme de fondateur se trouve maintenant aussi répandu que la faculté de conduire une automobile.*' Dom Jean-Baptiste Porion, *Lettres et écrits spirituels*, ed. Nathalie Nabert (Paris: Beauchesne, 2012), p. 470.

118 Cf. the end of the third chapter of the *Charter of Charity*: '*in actibus nostris nulla sit discordia, sed una caritate, una regula similibusque vivamus moribus*'.